TOWARD MARITAL BLISS

A 21-DAY MARRIAGE DEVOTIONAL FOR WOMEN

Gwendolene N.T. Mawoko (BBS, MBS, D.MIN)

FOREWORD

A solid, happy, fulfilling, and godly marriage is what God has ordained and desires for all. But this is not always the case because of attacks from the devil, who hates this godly institution, and mankind's ignorance and lack of wisdom in maintaining marriages. This book, *Toward Marital Bliss: A 21-Day Marriage Devotional for Women*, provides wisdom to improve one's marriage and answer many questions you may have.

The author, Gwen, is my spiritual daughter whom I have seen grow and mature from the time she was a newlywed and became Chairperson of Gracious Women's Fellowship in Victoria Falls, Zimbabwe, until she became a missionary together with her husband, Tad. She and her husband have counselled many couples and have saved some marriages that were on the verge of divorce. We have entrusted Gwen and Tad to teach on marriage on our TV station, Ezekiel TV. For several years they have held several successful Married Couples Retreats and many premarital counseling classes for those couples preparing to marry, equipping them to enter holy matrimony with some knowledge, wisdom, and an idea of what to expect. Gwendolene's marriage has been exemplary for 31 years.

It is my hope that you, the reader, as a wife or soon-to-be wife, will profit,be blessed and be enlightened as you glean from these God-inspired devotions for 21 days. May God speak to you and minister to you deeply as you read this devotional. God bless you and your marriage.

Apostle Dr. Eunor Guti (D. Min; PhD)
Archbishop, Director ZAOGA-FIF Women's Ministry,
Author, Marriage Counsellor

TESTIMONIALS

My family and I migrated to Australia full of hope and dreams, but they quickly dissipated as we were confronted with challenges of living in the diaspora. There were tensions and frustrations in my marriage, which required urgent attention. We did not want to seek help, so we had to maintain the façade that everything was great.

A miracle in disguise, we began fellowshipping with Pastors Gwen and Tad, and I began to glean from Gwen's wise counsel and dynamic marriage seminars. My husband and I were brought up in traditional churches and initially found it confronting to discuss our marital challenges, especially sexual matters, in the church. However, through their relentless love for successful marriages, their experience, gifts, integrity, and transparency, our holy matrimony was transformed to the blissful marriage of twenty-eight years we have today. I can honestly testify that this book is long overdue, as Pastors Tad and Gwen carry a wealth of knowledge, undisputable anointing, and honorable lifestyle of love.

Lydia Washaya
MBA (University of Queensland), BSW (University Newcastle), BPoliScAdmin (University of Zimbabwe), Grad. Dip. in Marketing Management, Dip. in Personal Management

Pastors Tad and Gwen have been our personal friends and co-workers for years. Their marriage has been a role model to many, and for Dr. Gwen to come up with this amazing devotional does not come as a surprise but as a fulfillment of their God-given purpose and mandate to impact marriages. God bless you, Dr. Gwen, for being obedient to open your life and experiences for the sake of many marriages. My three daughters and I will greatly benefit from this book. OCYC (Of Course You Can)!

Rudo Rwizi
Bachelor of Arts (English and Philosophy major) (UZ), Graduate certificate in Education (Educational Psychology major) (UZ), Applied Behavior Therapy (UF), Diploma in Pastoral Leadership (AMFCC),
Author of *My Pastor's Wife*

My husband and I have been married for thirteen years and have been privileged to have attended couples retreats and seminars where Dr. Gwen and Dr. Tad have ministered. Their teachings are God-centered and practical. From their teachings on marriage, we have learned the importance of communication, knowing how to love your spouse, managing family relationships, and love and respect. I thank God for using them mightily in this ministry as our marriage has been strengthened through their teachings

Dr Tafadzwa Nyanhanda
PhD, BScDN (Senior Lecturer in Public Health)

....

As a young wife and mother married for five years so far, I learned a lot about marriage from this book. I wish this book had been available before I got married, as I am convinced it would have added so much to the foundation of my marriage. My life has been transformed especially on how to approach my marriage. The generation we are in is ever ready to ditch marriage when faced with challenges, but this book will guide you and take away the overwhelming feeling of failure. As I read it, I felt like I had a counsellor who will not let go of you until you make it. It felt like I had a coach and trainer who took me through to the finish line as I was on a marathon with many roadblocks. Every topic is interconnected, and I love that it is full of Scripture. I will be recommending this book to every woman young and old who wants to experience a fulfilling marriage. What I love more about this devotional is that as I have spent time with Dr. Gwen, what she is teaching is what she practices.

Rudo Mutsigwa
MHA (LaTrobe University), BHSc (Deakin University), GradDipPsych (Swinburne University)
CEO- El-Roi Investments (Furniture Design & Sales, Recruitment Services, Grocery Supplies), Author, Motivational Speaker, FEN Coordinator)

....

As I am in my first year of marriage, I found the teachings in this book to be real and practical, addressing a number of issues that couples encounter in marriage.
This devotional will inspire many women like myself to continue fighting for their marriages. I found the Activity section of the devotional to be valuable as it forced me to reflect a lot on myself and how I handle issues in my own marriage. Thank you for encouraging women not to quit but to fight hard and work on their married lives. "Of Course You Can" (OCYC), as you say in your devotional, was such a timely reminder that as a woman I can have the best marriage and reach out for my dreams in my marriage and life. Thank you, Dr. Gwen. This is a must read for every woman who desires to have an amazing marriage.

Dr. Anna Paraffin-Samatepo
PhD AniSc (UKZN), M. AgriStudies (University of Queensland), BSc Nursing Sciences (Honors)(USC), BScAgriAniSc (UZ), National Cert. in Quality System Management

....

The way Dr. Gwen has written this book with constant references to the Bible makes one feel anchored in the advice they are receiving. Being a Christian woman while reading this book, I started to feel that it is okay not to be perfect all the time. The book addresses marriage from the start and through the journey. I have just celebrated my fifteenth year in marriage. Each chapter resonates depending on what part of the journey one is at, making it a book you keep for life. I loved the activities and check-ins at the end of each chapter, giving me the opportunity to pause and look in the mirror. This book challenges me to want to do better. Well done!

Linda Dunduru
BCom (Finance), Businesswoman, Entrepreneur, Franchisor

....

TOWARD MARITAL BLISS

A 21-DAY MARRIAGE DEVOTIONAL FOR WOMEN

Gwendolene N.T. Mawoko (BBS, MBS, D.MIN)

Published in Australia by REVIVE MEDIA
Postal: PO Box 1361 Fitzroy North , Victoria 3068, Australia,
Tel: +61 415 172 598/ +61 431 166 093
Email: gwen@tadandgwen.com
Website: www.tadandgwen.com

First published in Australia 2021
Copyright © Gwendolene N.T Mawoko 2021

All rights reserved. No part of this publication may be reproduced, stored in a retrieval system, or transmitted, in any form or by any means without the prior written permission of the publisher, nor be otherwise circulated in any form of binding or cover other than that in which it is published and without a similar condition being imposed on the subsequent purchaser.

National Library of Australia Cataloguing –in –
Publication entry

 A catalogue record for this book is available from the National Library of Australia

ISBN: # (paperback)   978-0-6450145-0-1
ISBN: # (hardback)   978-0-6450145-1-8
ISBN: # (epub)   978-0-6450145-2-5

Cover photography by THEOPHILUS MUTSIGWA

Printed by **Revive Media**

Disclaimer
All care has been taken in the preparation of the information herein, but no responsibility can be accepted by the publisher or author for any damages resulting from the misinterpretation of this work. All contact details given in this book were current at the time of publication, but are subject to change.

The advice given in this book is based on the experience of the individuals. Professionals should be consulted for individual problems. The author and publisher shall not be responsible for any person with regard to any loss or damage caused directly or indirectly by the information in this book.

DEDICATION

I dedicate this devotional to all married women and those who are about to marry. I further dedicate it to you, the woman who has worked hard to keep your marriage going through all the hardships and pain. There were many times it was easier to give up, but you did not. May your hard work be rewarded. I also dedicate this book to the woman who has always wondered whether other women are going through the same situations as you, juggling everything as a wife, mother, homemaker, home nurse, cook, maid, homeschool teacher, career woman, and for some, minister of the gospel or community leader. May the good Lord and Savior help you to maintain and balance it all—and triumph!

To my two wonderful, beautiful daughters, Pastor Bethany Ropafadzo Nothando (the Fashion Guru cum Pastor) and Belinda Anenyasha Nandi, Youth Leader and aspiring children's protection lawyer and psychologist. A mother could not ask for daughters more committed to God and to serving their generation. To my son, Bethel Tinashe Dumisani, whom the Lord will soon bless with a God-fearing wife, this devotional is for you and her. May your love for God only increase! Mom loves you beyond words!

Lastly but not least, I dedicate this book to every woman who has decided to allow God, through His Son Jesus Christ and the power of the Holy Spirit, to reign in your life and marriage. You have decided to surrender it all to Him, so He completely guides you and will fight your battles! Grace, grace, and more grace!

CONTENTS

DAY 1: *WHICH BUILDER ARE YOU WITH?*   1
    Allow God to build your marriage

DAY 2: *THE ART OF COMMUNICATION, PART 1*   4
    Viewing things from the 'Vantage Point'

DAY 3: *THE ART OF COMMUNICATION, PART 2*   10
    Communication Killers

DAY 4: *DEAL WITH INNER WOUNDS*   16
    Healing from Past Hurts

DAY 5: *MARRIAGE IS ABOUT TWO IMPERFECT PEOPLE*   20
    Marriage's Different Stages

Day 6: *SEEKING TO UNDERSTAND AND NOT JUDGE*   29
    Embracing My Man

DAY 7: *DYING PRINCIPLE*   35
    Getting Rid of Me, Myself, and I

DAY 8: *ALPHA MALE HIGHEST*   40
    My "A" Man

DAY 9: *PRIORITISING YOUR SPOUSE*   44
    My Numero Uno: #NBR 1

DAY 10: *LORDSHIP VS. LOVE*   48
    Recognizing His Respect Language

DAY 11: *DO NOT TAKE EACH OTHER FOR GRANTED*   54
    Serving Him My Best

DAY 12: *WITH MY BODY I HONOR YOU*   57
    Let's Get it On, Babe

DAY 13: *LET'S DO LIFE TOGETHER*   62
    "Us" Moments

DAY 14: *SURPRISE GIFTS*   66
    Gestures of Love

DAY 15: *AUTHORISED DEALER*   70
    Guard Your Turf

DAY 16: *SELF-CARE*   75
      Thou Shall Love Thyself

DAY 17: *FROM IN-LAWS TO IN-LOVES*   80
      Your People Shall Be My People

Day 18: *VIEWING HIM THROUGH THE WORD*   85
      Word-Based 'P' Pillars

DAY 19: *DIFFERENT WIRING*   91
      Difference in Wiring Brings Excitement

DAY 20: *KEEP SWEET MEMORIES ALIVE*   96
      Good Times Last Forever in Our Hearts

DAY 21: *QUITTING IS NOT AN OPTION*   100
      Of Course You Can (OCYC

INTRODUCTION

The vision to write this devotional came as we were in our 30th year of marriage. Surrounded by the busy lifestyle of balancing family, ministry, and life in general, we were enjoying our time together until one Friday night when we got into a huge disagreement—what my husband and I call an "intense moment of fellowship." This fellowship was indeed intense! The timing was terrible. We were on our way to a church leadership seminar, so we decided to revisit our reason for the misunderstanding and "intense fellowship" after the service because we realized that there was something more to the dispute than what was on the surface.

We created time to talk and came to a place of listening and understanding each other. During our discussion, we realized that a few things had changed in our lives. We had both slackened on how to treat each other well, and this needed restoration, repair, and renewal. We noted how we were now taking each other for granted and not prioritizing each other's needs. We vowed to each other not to ever get into that rut and place of broken communication ever again. This is what led me to writing this devotional as a reminder, lest we forget to cherish each other every step of the way. I began to sense the urging of the Holy Spirit to quickly put what He was showing me to paper. So, I started jotting down topics, themes, and teachings as the Holy Spirit revealed, which culminated in this book.

As I write this devotional, I am well aware that it takes two to tango. A marriage cannot work through the input of the wife alone, without the man responding accordingly and doing his part to make it work. Each husband must treat his wife right, be a representative of Jesus in the marriage, and love his wife as Christ loved the church. However, in 30 years of marriage counseling, I have seen my fair share of ladies who have literally sabotaged their marriages and lost good husbands because of ignorance, stubbornness, or spiritual influence (anti-marriage demons).

Furthermore, many ladies are getting into marriage without premarital counseling. I hope this book is not too late for your marriage. In studying the

Bible, I am yet to see a man who influenced his wife in a major way, but there are several examples of women who influenced their husbands effectively . . . either for good or for bad. This shows me that we, as women, are powerful. We are creatures of serious influence and if our influence is positive, focused, and intelligently informed and applied with prayer, we can surely influence our husbands and change situations in our marriages forever, thus realizing marital bliss.

As a Christian woman, I have thoroughly enjoyed my marriage. Incidences like the one mentioned above leading to "intense moments of fellowship" have been far and wide in my marriage. True, some incidences have been tough and taxing, but through what I am sharing in this book, such incidences were soon over in a day. With this knowledge and grace upon my marriage, I have managed to counsel scores and scores of women successfully. My husband and I have won back many marriages that had broken down, including couples who were separated with divorce papers in the courts waiting for a court date or the signatures.

I have been fortunate and blessed to be in a church organization (Forward in Faith Ministries International) that holds marriage in high regard and teaches on it tirelessly. My husband and I both come from broken families, so neither of us can claim to have seen an example of a good marriage from our parents. Both of our fathers abandoned our mothers and the families. Tad's dad left when Tad was about five years old, and mine went MIA (Missing in Action) when I was in high school. I was remarkably close to him, so it was very painful. But all this did not stop me from having a blissful marriage. I decided when Tad and I were dating that in spite of my inner fears and insecurities brought by my parents' broken marriage, I was going to work on my marriage. I was determined that our marriage would not become a statistic for failure.

I will be the first to tell you that it has not been easy, especially where family members (his or mine) were involved. I did my part and thank God he did his part, and here we are! Apart from countless couple-by-couple or one-on-one counseling sessions, together we have held several one-day seminars and weekend retreats on marriage with resounding success and phenomenal feedback. God has allowed me to touch many ladies' lives and many marriages from the southern nations of Africa to USA, Canada, UK, New Zealand, and

Australia. As I write, we are privileged to have people who phone from overseas for marriage counseling and we have to do it over the phone, sometimes more than once per couple. They later phone back to say the problem is solved and they are happy. For this I give glory to God!

If a middle child from a broken marriage who married a middle child also from a broken marriage can have a blissful marriage full of victory, passion, love, and fun, my sister, you can have this, too!

As you read one chapter of this devotional per day, please read to the end of each chapter exercise, and take time to reflect. I suggest that you take your time. You could also decide to do one chapter per week if that suits you better. The idea is to allow each teaching to sink into your soul and allow it to transform you through meditation on it. Discussing with a friend who also holds marriage in high esteem will also benefit you. Aim to change accordingly or improve your present situation as the teaching of the day may direct. Be determined to let go of bad habits or anything that will hinder you from obtaining your marital bliss.

I trust the Spirit of God will reveal to you many things in your marriage and give you strength to overcome. May your marriage flourish and be full of love, trust, commitment, fun, peace, and good memories!

Marriage is for enjoying, not enduring!

DAY 1: WHICH BUILDER ARE YOU WITH?

While marriage is about two people who love each other, it is important to keep God at the center of each relationship, as He is the author of marriage and ordained the first marriage in the garden of Eden.

Psalm 127:1 says, "Unless the Lord builds the house, they labor in vain who build it. Unless the Lord guards the city, the watchman stays awake in vain."

Commit your house and marriage into God's hands and always acknowledge Him as the builder and creator of your life, with Jesus as the chief cornerstone. The written Word, the Bible, is the manual God has given us to help us flourish in our marriages. When the Word of God is accompanied by prayer as a way of communicating with the author of marriage, it enables us to be successful and to overcome the challenges that come our way.

Ecclesiastes 4:12 says, "Though one may be overpowered by another, two can withstand him. And a threefold cord is not quickly broken."
Keep the vertical relationship of prayer alive in your home and the horizontal relationship between the two of you will be strengthened.

Things you must always remember:

- Nothing moves without prayer.
- All your issues need to be presented to God.
- When you made your vows, you declared war on the enemy.
- The battle for your relationship started at the altar and it is maintained at the altar through prayer.
- Your marriage vows were declared at the marriage altar. Continue to take your marriage to the altar of prayer. Stay fervent in prayer, as the enemy is always looking for ways to destroy this God-ordained institution.

Do you believe that God brought you two together? Very often, we believe we have done things by our own strength. We must acknowledge that God brought us together as husband and wife. Surrender your marriage to God. He

is the great and original architect to build your home. The Bible is the blueprint given for our use.
Through intimacy with God, you can build greater intimacy with your husband. Time in the presence of God as one unit is a powerful weapon against the enemy.

Ben and Tangeni's Story

Ben and Tangeni came to us for help. They had significant marital problems and quarreled all the time. Ben loved his wife but was about to give up. He had grown up in church, but when he married Tangeni she was not a believer and they clashed every day. We managed to let Tangeni know that handling marriage her own way would not help. She needed God to guide her. Because she also loved her husband, she agreed to accept Jesus in her life and allow Him to rule her marriage. With teaching, their marriage changed from the brink of divorce. That was over 22 years ago. They are still happily married and running successful businesses.

ACTIVITY

Practical Steps: Exercise on Building Your House God's Way

1) Prayer here is defined as: Acknowledging God in thought or words as the master builder of your house.
How often do you pray for your marriage or read the Word of God together?
   1. Not often enough
   2. Often, depending on our schedule
   3. We have a scheduled routine.
   4. Average
   5. Great (almost perfect)

2) Another great way of bonding is around Scripture.
   ➢ Try doing Bible quizzes and games together.
   ➢ Have Scripture hanging around the house.
   ➢ Learn your spouse's favorite Scripture passage.
   ➢ Learn each other's favorite praise or worship song.

ENCOURAGEMENT

Develop a routine that works for you with your schedule to enhance your spiritual life together. In life we will meet difficult times and sad days, but through praying together the pain will be bearable and we can overcome.

REFLECTION

_____
_____
_____
_____
_____
_____
_____
_____
_____
_____
_____
_____
_____
_____
_____
_____
_____
_____
_____

#FamilyThatPraysTogetherStaysTogether

DAY 2: THE ART OF COMMUNICATION, PART 1

Communication in a marriage is vital and can be compared to blood in the body. A couple that can communicate well can overcome obstacles and reduce friction in the home. Our words have the power to create peace or cause havoc. Scripture says, *"Death and life are in the power of the tongue, and those who love it will eat its fruit" (Proverbs 18:21).* This reminds us to watch what we say to each other.

In any war, the enemy knows that the best way to defeat their opponent is to cut off their communication line or to hijack it and send mixed signals or confusing instructions. This is the same strategy the devil attempts to use in our marriages. In *2 Corinthians 2:11 we read, "Lest Satan should take advantage of us; for we are not ignorant of his devices (schemes)."*

Healthy communication is a pillar to a wholesome marriage. Every marriage goes through turbulence, challenges, and problems. How we communicate and resolve these challenges determines the health of our marriage.

1) There are simple, basic ground rules of engagement to foster open communication in the home. Here are some big NO GO areas in our communication. In a boxing ring, these would be equated to hitting below the belt and in a soccer match, a player would get a red card for such misconduct.

Please note the following:

- no shouting; reduce the volume.
- no cursing, bad language, or swear words.
- no threats or language of intimidation
- no throwing phrases like "I will divorce you"
- no name calling.
- no sarcasm, disrespect, or pulling each other down. This can be a sign of something deeper that should be worked on and done away with.

Yes, I know this sounds like work. Marriage is work, but if you put in the work, you will enjoy the fruit. This is a process that we can go through together and overcome.

2) There are also nonverbal expressions that should not be found between two people who love each other, such as banging doors, rolling eyes, folding hands, or shrugging shoulders, to name a few. My aim is to work on not using any of these, as they are a barrier or hindrance to excellent communication. Men and women look for different things in communication. Men seek to be respected in any communication that we might engage in, while women typically want to hear security and affection.

3) Our communication can also be affected by our character, as some are introverts (quiet, reserved, and thoughtful), and others are extroverts (energized, vocally expressive, and talkative around other people). While opposites may attract in courtship, if there is lack of proper communication in marriage, these differences can be the cause of many misunderstandings.

Where matters must be addressed, learn to speak the truth in love. Using mercy without truth is like a cheerleader without a team. Truth must be accompanied with mercy, otherwise on its own it is like putting someone in surgery without an anesthesia. Learn to give each other the right to speak the truth in a loving way. It is not only what you say, but how you say it.

Addressing the truth with mercy means that we still want to live together but we must tackle the problem we are facing and resolve it peacefully. When a couple does not tell each other the truth but rather hides away from each other, it can create a cold war situation in the home. Be transparent with each other.

There are different types of communication, but I have realized that "the Ezekiel Type of Communication" is one of the best methods in communication.

THE EZEKIEL TYPE OF COMMUNICATION

In this type of communication, you put yourself in your spouse's shoes and seek to see and understand things from their point of view in order to respond with empathy, understanding, insight, and compassion. You view your challenges from "The Vantage Point," a place or position affording the best view to a situation or problem in the family or with your spouse. *Ezekiel 3:15-16 says, "Then I came to the captives at Tel Abib, who dwelt by the River Chebar; and I sat where they sat and remained there astonished among them seven days. Now it came to pass at the end of seven days that the word of the Lord came to me, saying . . . ."*

Before Ezekiel prophesied to the captives at the River Chebar, he put himself in their shoes. He "sat where they sat" and felt their pain, anguish, loss, and anxiety. Only then did he begin to prophesy and speak, addressing them at their point of need. If we learn to put ourselves in each other's shoes, we are far more likely to respond with love, patience, and tolerance to the many challenges we encounter in the home.

Care about your spouse with the language you use. I recall counseling a young lady who admitted, "I think I have verbal diarrhea." This is when one just spews words without realizing the damage they are doing. In that counseling session, we emphasized the importance of being mindful of the words we speak. This Ezekiel method of communication is a good cure. Assess your words before you speak.

Felix and Pauline's Story
When we took over a certain assembly as its new pastors, the outgoing pastors warned us about Felix and Pauline, a couple who were in the church who would verbally fight every month. This routine continued until Pauline eventually moved out to her own rental apartment with the children. Everybody thought this was now the end of the marriage. However, after a thorough counseling session, Pauline realized that she still loved her husband and wanted him to come and join her at the new place. We brought the husband in, who came to the counseling meeting reluctantly. After a "no holds barred" conversation, we realized the major issue was communication. Pauline would throw hurtful words, and when the husband retaliated, she would cry foul and react extremely. We had to point out to Pauline to speak civilly to Felix. Felix had a list of bad words and statements Pauline used to say to him. I took Pauline aside and shared with her the basics of communication with her husband. She promised to change, and change she did.

This was over 18 years ago, and they are still together, happy and serving God in the ministry.

ACTIVITY

Practical Steps: Exercise on the Art of Communication

- Find out from your spouse what makes him tick and what makes him ticked off.
- What negative body language do I need to get rid of?
- List your strengths in communication.
- Verbalize your appreciation for your spouse and let him know you treasure him. No deed is too small for some acknowledgement.
- How do you rate yourself on a scale of 1 to 5 for the following questions?
    a) Am I a good listener?
    b) Do I have empathy when something is being explained?
    c) Do I apply the Ezekiel Method of Communication?

ENCOURAGEMENT

In our marriage, we have agreed to not go to bed angry at each other. This has helped us learn to quickly resolve any disagreements and not hold on to grudges. It helps us to start each new day on a clean slate and it keeps our marriage fresh.

REFLECTION

#KeepCommunicationLineOpen

DAY 3: THE ART OF COMMUNICATION, PART 2

COMMUNICATION KILLERS

When I got married, my father warned my husband that he was marrying "the water works," and rightfully so. As a child growing up, I would cry to get my way, to control, and to manipulate—and it worked. Through my tears, I had my parents wrapped around my finger. I was not aware that in marriage, that method of communicating which bullies and intimidates one's spouse would not work. During the first year of our marriage, I attempted to use the water works every time my husband tried to correct or highlight any mistake I made. Then one day he sat me down with a box of tissues and said, "You can cry, but we need to address this matter." That was the end of me using tears to control.

Sometimes we use other behaviors without being aware that they are affecting our communication in the home. At times, these behaviors can even push your spouse away. For this reason it's important to do some introspection, acknowledge our weaknesses, then get on the path toward positive change.

Communication Barriers

Here are some of the communication killers, barriers, and hindrances we may need to address:

1) Fear of Rejection

If I voice my honest opinion, what will my spouse do or say? How will they react? Fear of being ridiculed, judged, or of the information being used against me can hinder free communication. In *1 John 4:18, the Bible says, "There is no fear in love; but perfect love casts out fear . . . ."* Therefore, in our communication we should be honest with one another. There must be integrity in our speech. *Proverbs 10:9 says, "He who walks with integrity walks securely . . . ." Proverbs 20:7 says, "The righteous man walks in his integrity . . . ."* Integrity is more important than fear of rejection.

2) The Messiah Mask Lifestyle

This begins by being there for everyone and everything else except your spouse. It's when you become an angel at church and to all other people, yet at home you are a monster in the way you conduct yourself. You put on a mask for all to see you as a kind, patient, and understanding person, but the minute you are home you remove the mask and show your true self. This leaves your spouse confused as to who you really are. Charity begins at home. Let us do good starting from home first, then allow that good to overflow to outside people.

3) Volcanic Response

This is a violent response one gives when things do not go their way, or when one is being corrected. *Proverbs 15:1 says, "A soft answer turns away wrath, but a harsh word stirs up anger." Proverbs 29:11 says, "A fool vents all his feelings but a wise man holds them back."* Shouting, temper tantrums, intimidation, etc. are volcanic responses. Some people use this trick when their spouse is getting too close to the truth of something wrong that the guilty party is doing. It is a cover-up tactic. Their action is sending the signal, "Do not get too close, do not address this, keep quiet." They use it to control or manipulate their spouse.

4) The Water Works

This was my weakness, and thank God He delivered me. Truly a human being is a redeemable creature. I was set free from the spirit of controlling and manipulation. At the bottom of it, I did not want my husband to tell me the truth about my mistakes. For us to live together in peace, we must address the elephant in the room. We cannot keep sweeping things under the rug. Soon the rug will not be able to hide it. Manipulation is the weapon of a control freak. Nobody wants to be controlled or dominated by another person.

5) The Silent Treatment

This is mostly used by someone who has passive anger or passive aggression. They go on mute, curl up like a tortoise in its shell, and refuse to talk. We once counseled a couple where the husband would use this method if he felt that he was not heard in any matter in the home. The wife said, "Pastor, this silence is deafening and more painful because you do not know what he is thinking or what his next move will be." She expressed how it would put real fear in her as if she was in danger, only she did not know what kind of danger she might be in.

If the silent treatment has been happening in your home, it's time get help and stop inflicting pain on the ones we love. Some use this tactic because they do not want to explode as they think its ungodly, but silence is equally wrong as it does not solve anything. Bottling up anger can lead to sickness. So, do yourself a favor: open your mouth and talk.

Communication can be grouped into these different percentages: 17% tone of voice, 53% body language, 23% other things, like eye contact. We must be aware of the signals we are sending to our spouses and the messages we are sending with our tone of voice and body gestures. As stated above, the biggest percentage is the non-verbal communication, which comprises of banging doors, pulling feet when walking, sitting quietly without responding, rolling eyes, folding hands, etc. Always remember that a human being is a spirit; you may not open your mouth, but one may sense that something is not right.

Here are some more "No Go" areas. No matter how heated the argument gets, pinching, punching, pulling, and shoving are strictly not allowed. Physical abuse does not solve anything, but rather worsens the situation. Do not raise your hand or voice in communication. My spouse should not associate my hand with a "weapon of mass destruction." Rather, my hand must be associated with caressing, massaging, and bringing pleasure, not pain. Ladies, remember our husbands are not mind readers. Let's respectfully express our concerns in the home so that we do not become moody. My aim is not to judge you, but to make you aware that these kinds of behaviors affect our marriages. We are all a work in progress. Acknowledging one's weaknesses is the first step to improving and being a better person to live with.

EXPECTATIONS
When we get married, we both have realistic and unrealistic expectations. Communicate your expectations. Work on making the realistic realm and toss out the unrealistic ones—otherwise you'll get frustrated in your marriage. Remember, marriage is not Hollywood; its real life. Let's be real.

Kevin and Jane's Story

Jane had the habit of giving her husband Kevin the silent treatment whenever she thought he had wronged her. Sometimes she was right that Kevin had messed up, but the silent treatment was not the way to solve the problem. Kevin called it "Silent Hell" and needed some intervention. We encouraged Jane not to bottle up her feelings and make life hell for her husband, but to speak up and get things sorted out. When Jane began to verbalize her concerns and not harbor ill feelings, the marriage turned around completely.

ACTIVITY

Practical Steps: Exercise to Avoid Communication Killers

- ◆ The marriage should be a safe zone.
- ◆ The first step is to identify one's weaknesses.
- ◆ Talk about it with your spouse.
- ◆ If you need outside help for deliverance or anger management, get help.
- ◆ Exercise self-control.

ENCOURAGEMENT

"When you have a minute, honey, I have something I need your advice on." In our marriage, this line usually means I have something important or sensitive to discuss and I need my spouse's undivided attention. Then we both prepare to tackle any subject without judging each other. Find a way that works for you to prepare each other for difficult conversations.

REFLECTION

#SafeZoneMarriage

DAY 4: DEAL WITH INNER WOUNDS

*H*urt people hurt others. If you've been hurt, allow God to take you through the process of healing. Healing is a process that God can walk you through so you can give the best of yourself to those you love.

Let's consider Saul's daughter, Michal:

Background Verses:
> *1 Samuel 14:49 - described as daughter of Saul*
> *1 Samuel 18:20-28*
> *1 Samuel 19:9-17 - saves David from Saul*
> *1 Samuel 25:44 - given to Palti as wife*
> *2 Samuel 3:13-16 - David demands her from Abner*

The story of Michal in the Bible depicts a woman who had been through a lot in life and perhaps had not taken time to deal with her inner wounds and hurts from past experiences. She was given to David in marriage as her father was trying to set a trap for David by asking for the foreskins of the Philistines. This may have opened a door to daddy issues, since he used her as a trap. Fathers are usually the first male figure a girl encounters in life. Saul literally sold Michal to David, who succeeded in bringing the requested bridal price and married her.

Saul was still after David when Michal lied to save his life, showing that she obviously loved him. David ran away and Michal was given in marriage to another man called Palti, like a piece of property.

After some time, David asked to have her back and Palti cried behind her as she was taken away from him, but she did not cry. She finds herself back in David's arms and bed but by then David had brought in other women, which was lawful at that time.

Her story ends with her lashing out at the King of Israel as he was bringing the Ark of the Covenant to Jerusalem. Everyone saw a godly, humble King dancing before God, but she despised him and viewed him as showing off to the daughters of Israel. In 2 Samuel 6:16 she ridicules David and as a result becomes barren. Barrenness was the price she paid for the hurts she was harboring in her heart.

You cannot enjoy something you despise! Everyone saw the king in David while Michal did not. How do you view your husband? Watch it, because you will speak it out. From the abundance of the heart the mouth will speak. Once words come out, they cannot go back; the damage is done. It cost Michal intimacy with her husband. She became barren (unfruitful, be it spiritually or physically). The Bible says she never had any children after that. Some believe David never slept with her again. Could it be that intimacy was killed by her actions? Some lessons in life are better learned from the mistakes of others.

Gina's Story

My husband and I once counseled a woman named Gina, who was in a very abusive relationship. After trying her best to hold on, she was thrown out into the street by her mean husband. The abuse she endured was verbal, emotional, economical, and physical.

Counseling helped Gina to stand on her own until a few years later when a great young man proposed to her. As much as she had fallen in love with this man, she was very hesitant, as she was often reminded of her previous marriage. She had to come to the realization that she could start afresh, that she had the right to be in love and happy again. Regular counseling helped her so that by the wedding day she was free of any baggage and would not punish the new, loving husband for the sins of her ex-husband.

ACTIVITY

Practical Steps: Exercise for Healing from Hurts

- Identify what or who it is that hurt you.
- Forgive yourself and any other person who was involved. Forgiving from the heart is key to your healing. Every act of forgiveness and letting go is an act of healing yourself. Ask the Lord to give you the strength and grace to forgive. Use the Word of God as your source of strength. Keep the joy of the Lord inside of you as you allow the Lord to heal you. ***Proverbs 17:22 says, "A merry heart doeth good like medicine; but a broken spirit driest the bones." See also Matthew 6:14-15.***
- Heal and detox from any toxins that contaminated you from past relationships.
- Cut off soul ties. There is nothing as sad as getting a good man after you have been through a bad one and making the good man pay for your ex's mistakes.
- Michal despised her own husband when he was bringing the Ark of God into Jerusalem. Ask yourself, "What is my response when my husband gets excited in the house of God or at any event? Do I join him in the celebrations, or due to hidden issues do I show negative body language or simply walk away?"

- Ask yourself, "Is there anything I have not forgiven him about?"
- Address the areas or events that led to the hurt, and forgive. Be prepared to also apologize if your spouse expresses areas you might have hurt him in the process. Do not allow pride to get in the way of healing.
- Enlist the help of a counselor whom you both trust and emulate their marriage.
- Allow Jehovah Rapha to heal your wounds.

ENCOURAGEMENT

One young lady I met rushed into the wrong hands in her love walk and married an abusive man. Her marriage was very rocky and full of victimization. One day her husband threw her out onto the street. She went through a nasty divorce. After years of rededicating her life back to the Lord, God brought a God-fearing man into her life and she remarried. One day she came to me privately and said, "Pastor, help me to embrace the love and care I am receiving from my husband." She needed to realize that not all men are like her ex. Like her, you deserve to be happy.

REFLECTION

_____

_____

_____

_____

_____

_____

#WoundCare

DAY 5: MARRIAGE IS ABOUT TWO IMPERFECT PEOPLE

Marriage is about two imperfect people coming together.

A story is told about a young couple who tightly held their hands together all during their courtship, on the day of their wedding, during the honeymoon, and into their early years in marriage. They simply could not keep their hands apart from each other because of the romantic feeling of the love bond. After their first and second children were born, they were seen at the mall still holding hands. This time it was to keep each other from straying into different shops and overspending as they now had a budget to adhere to. Life went on and years passed by until grandchildren came onto the scene. The same couple was seen holding hands at the park, this time even with a tighter grip and closer than ever before. Wow! Somebody asked their secret, and they said this time they were holding hands for balance, to help each other and to keep each other from falling. Lesson: Keep holding hands as you figure out life together.

Ecclesiastes 4:9-12 says, "Two are better than one . . . . If either of them falls, one can help the other up. But pity anyone who falls and has no one to help them up!" (paraphrased) We need each other.

Nobody is perfect, so stop trying to fix your spouse. We have already addressed how to communicate on things that are genuinely affecting your marriage and how to resolve conflict. But to pick on every wrong thing your spouse does and try to correct and fix it can be bordering on nagging or being a second mother. It is also so exhausting and energy sucking that you can end up with no strength for important issues. Just drop it, my dear. The way he chews or snores will not change any time soon, if at all.

Check out the following Scriptures:

- *Proverbs 19:13 – "A foolish son is the ruin of his father, and the contentions of a wife are a continual dripping."*
- *Proverbs 21:9 – "Better to dwell in a corner of a housetop, than in a house shared with a contentious woman."*
- *Proverbs 21:19 – "Better to dwell in the wilderness, than with a contentious and angry woman."*
- *Proverbs 27:15-16 – "A continual dripping on a very rainy day and a contentious woman are alike; whoever restrains her restrains the wind, and grasps oil with his right hand."*

In short, DON'T NAG!

Do not be your husband's second mom; it kills the romance in the marriage. Learn to let go. Save your gun powder for when you really need it. Do not fire off at anything and everything. Men have selective hearing; if you are constantly nagging at everything, he switches off. When you need him to listen to important, lifesaving ideas or information, he will be like, "Here we go again" and tune you out.

My husband and I have developed a way of addressing things that are genuinely affecting the marriage. Sometimes I will just say, "Sweetie, when you have a minute, I have something I need your input on." Then he will tell me when he is ready. That way, I have his attention and we talk and finish and move on.

I am reminded of Esther in the Bible and how she found a way for the golden scepter to be lifted in her favor because she had a pressing urgent issue and her husband, the King, ruled in her favor. He listened. My sister, there is a way to your husband's heart and for issues to be addressed without nagging. Differences are going to surface, and communication is the key to resolving them. Marriage is about two imperfect people coming together to become one. Hurdles will arise, but how you communicate will determine how happy and healthy your marriage will be.

Marriage vows include the statement, "For better for worse." Often we do not pay much attention until we get married, but really, we should have done some homework in courtship. However, we are now married and truly some people are good at hiding flaws in their life until they marry. This brings us to the different stages in marriage.

STAGES OF MARRIAGE

The Honeymoon Stage
This is the time where you are really head over heels in love and you see no wrong in your spouse. In your eyes, he is a knight in shining armor. He seems perfect and can do no wrong. However, we all know this is not how life will remain. After a while, you notice mistakes. As you grow more comfortable with each other, one's true colors begin to surface and reality sets in.

The Realistic Stage
Real life begins to happen when you get to the realistic stage – when your eyes begin to see the mistakes, the wrongs, the imperfections, and all the negatives about your spouse. This is when we need to be careful not to be abusive to each other. This

stage is necessary in a marriage. It is like a test that matures you and makes you better, not bitter.

Patience and tolerance can be low at this stage. Serious weaknesses begin to surface. If intervention is not found, the two of you can fall into the trap of speaking with disrespect to each other. Forgiving each other is crucial. Remember, you are to complement one another, not compete. Submission to one another is needed here for the ship to sail in peace. It is important to seek counsel in this season of marriage. Some even walk away thinking, "He is not the man I married." He is the man you married! A right partner is not a perfect partner. All you need now is the wisdom to pull through.

Proverbs 24:3-4 says, "Through wisdom a house is built and by understanding it is established, by knowledge the rooms are filled with all precious and pleasant riches." Your marriage will be established through your acting and speaking wisely. When times are tough, do not throw out the baby with the bath water. Remember, marriage is work. Are you willing to put in the work to enjoy tomorrow? Get counsel from people who have traveled that path before.

Titus 2:3-5 says, "[Teach] the older women likewise, that they be reverent in behavior, not slanderers, not given to much wine, teachers of good things, that they admonish the young women to love their husbands, to love their children, to be discreet, chaste, homemakers, good, obedient to their own husbands, that the word of God may not be blasphemed." Do not lose hope. With teaching and training, you will soon move to the next stage of marriage.

The Maturity Stage

This is when you have accepted that some things do not always change and have found a healthy way of going around them with a clean heart. Your love is rekindled, and this time with experience you know how to navigate life's ups and downs together. Unconditional love begins, and you are submitting without conditions. Agape love begins to flourish, and *1 Corinthians 13:1-7* starts to make more sense. Wisdom takes center stage. You learn to live in harmony with your spouse and your intimacy is revived.

Things to always remember:

➤ Now that you know his past, do not judge him; celebrate his strengths.
➤ Rub his ego the right way by:
a) complimenting him on his looks or strengths.
b) remind him how important he is in your life.
c) doing the little personal things on his heart.

Top Tip: Just like a woman, a man wants to feel that if you could do it all over again, you would still choose him.

Jane's Story

Jane was a perfectionist, especially when it came to housekeeping. Even with a husband and two children, she expected to see her house in top notch order whenever she came back from work. Having moved to a new country, her husband was still in between jobs but was very good in helping with the children, bathing them, doing homework with them, and cooking for them and his wife.

However, when Jane came home from work every evening, the kitchen was always a mess, but there was her loving husband smiling from ear to ear and boasting that the kids were already in bed, fed, and bathed and her dinner was in the oven. Jane came secretly to me, complaining about the heap of dirty dishes and the mess in the kitchen every night. I helped her see that her imperfect husband was missing it on the dishes, but she had to be grateful she was coming home to a hot meal and she didn't have to do kids' homework or start to prepare a meal. She realized this and was glad, and began appreciating her husband more.

ACTIVITY

Practical Steps: Excercise for Two Imperfect People

A) Get to know him better.
Having knowledge regarding the topics below will help you learn how to better deal with your spouse. A big part of who we are is decided by these factors.

1. What is his birth order? Is he the first born, last born, or middle child?
2. What are his parents' personality types?
3. What was his childhood like? Who were the closest people in his life? (Sister, brother, grandma, best friend, etc.)
4. What was socio-economic background?
5. Where and how was he raised?
6. What is his personality type?
7. What is his temperament?

B) Build on his strengths.

1. What are my weak areas that are affecting your marriage? Yes, it takes two to tango.
2. Remember the phrase from your marriage vows, "For better for worse." Make a list of the "better" or the good qualities in each other. Compile another list of the "worse" or bad qualities; in other words, the issues you still need to improve on. Then make a conscious intentional plan on how to work on those shortcomings.

C) Focus on areas of improvement.
1. Strengthening your marriage is a process, not an overnight work.
2. Pray and find the right time to bring up any weaknesses that may be affecting your relationship, then choose your words with wisdom.
3. Remember the guidelines on communication (truth must be accompanied with mercy; on its own, it is like performing an operation on someone without anesthetic).
4. Use the sandwich approach in your communication (i.e. positive – negative – positive). Mention how the issue is affecting you without accusing your spouse. No pointing of fingers or blaming each other.

ENCOURAGEMENT
Reaching the maturity stage was not without its challenges in our marriage. We now laugh at the times we would allow things and people to get between the two of us. I remember the time when even our own children were in their teens and would always want to separate us by using us against each other. Then one day we saw that we needed to have one voice, even when it came to our own kids. Raising teenagers brought us even closer together.

REFLECTION

#NotForTheFaintHearted

DAY 6: SEEKING TO UNDERSTAND AND NOT JUDGE

As we journey together in marriage, we may find that the pressures of life can get in the way. We need to be careful not to allow these pressures to separate us, especially as we go through different stages and circumstances of life, one of which is midlife crisis. Midlife crises often catch a lot of couples unaware. They begin to think their spouse has changed and do not understand how or why. Because the toll is heavier on the man, you may notice that he is behaving strangely.

This is a normal stage of life that most men go through. His body starts to deteriorate, and he begins to feel trapped by marriage, work, and other responsibilities of life. He becomes more aware of unreached goals socially, academically, and materially. Without the intervention of a good mentor or other wise counsel, most men make unwise, costly mistakes at this time which can cost them financially or relationally. He begins to think the grass is greener on the other side. It is like he wants to prove that he can still catch a beautiful woman. Beware of the devil's trap of adultery in this time.

1 Kings 15:5 shows how King David had a "Bathsheba moment of weakness" and committed the sin of adultery. Remember, **Hebrews 13:4 says, "Marriage is honorable among all, and the marriage bed undefiled; but fornicators and adulterers God will judge."** It's best to be vigilant about our marriage during this stage and exercise a lot of self-control and self-discipline to guard our marriage from any outside predators.

Family responsibilities weigh heavily on men, and your spouse may feel like he is drowning. He has no time for himself due to his hectic schedule, and becomes very susceptible and vulnerable. He finds it hard to communicate freely. His heart weighs heavy inside and he may begin to make almost juvenile decisions, like buying a fast, expensive motor-bike or an expensive sports car on credit.

When my husband went through this stage, I noticed the changes but did not know how to handle it. He was investing money into a project in which I knew he was being cheated. The more I wanted to make him aware that he was going to lose money, the more he was adamant that it was the right decision. I prayed, yes, and spoke with him. However, this stage requires divine intervention. Eventually, after losing quite a lot of hard-earned family money, my husband's eyes were opened.

I thank God that this only happened once, and we have since recovered and I have long forgiven him. I had to make a choice to love my husband and continue to respect him and realize that money cannot come between us. Our bond is stronger than money, and that was our test. He has since made some financially profitable decisions.

Do not give up on your man during this stage. It requires long-suffering and much patience. Seek counsel and get help. Remember, it is a stage that will pass. It requires a wise woman not to quit. Reassure him of your undying love for him. Words of affirmation and appreciation of the hard work he does go a long way in helping him to stay focused on his family. It is also in this season that both spouses can feel sandwiched by pressures. Our parents are ailing, getting old, and becoming more if not totally dependent on us financially and emotionally. Some are dying on us even after we've done our best to keep them alive. You are working harder trying to catch up, sending money here, there, and everywhere, investing, paying the mortgage and bills . . . the list is endless. Chasing goals and upgrading our education is great, but everything must be done in moderation.

We may find ourselves playing taxi driver for our high school children, who are fully dependent on us for transportation to and from all the extracurricular activities. Once our children hit their teens and begin to run circles around us, you may feel like a captain who has lost control of his ship. As young adults they begin to make their own decisions, but still run to you when met with the consequences of their wrong decisions. They want to rebel, and you are on guard 24/7 trying to knock sense into them. They drain you emotionally and financially (some think parents are a living ATM). After college they get married and leave the two of you where you began, except now with less energy.

Remember, kids grow and leave the nest, but spouses must still live together. Often couples drift apart during this season. Research done in Europe has shown that couples are divorcing after retirement because now that the kids have left the nest and the husband and wife are no longer going to work, they are spending more time together at home but discover they have nothing in common. Their worlds drifted apart during the working years. Each spouse had a dear friend at work whom they confided in, but now they are both stuck at home together and irritating each other to a divorce.

Stand By Your Man

A woman holds the key to the stability and productivity of men (from George Gilder, the brilliant sociologist). When a wife believes in her husband and deeply respects him, he gains the confidence necessary to compete successfully and live responsibly.

By standing by her man, a woman gives her husband a reason to:

- Harness his masculine energy
- Build a home
- Obtain and keep a job
- Run a business
- Actively participate in the raising of children
- Remain sober and vigilant
- Live within the law of the land and the Word of God
- Spend and invest money wisely
- Focus on his family
- Be a responsible citizen

Without positive feminine influence, a man's tendency is to release the power of testosterone in a way that is destructive to himself and to society at large. Create a safe zone that encourages him. Do not give up on him or be tempted to say negative words. Remain positive.

Olivia's Story

A sister called Olivia in the USA once testified, "I will not leave my husband and allow another woman to take him. I have worked too hard for him to be where he is. I can't leave another woman to enjoy my sweat." Determination is a marriage goal. Love and wisdom will win the day. Stand by your man. If you do not see eye-to-eye, then walk hand-in-hand until the vision is clear.

ACTIVITY

Practical Steps: Exercise to Grow in Understanding and Not Judge or Attack

- Seek a wise counselor that you both agree on.
- Have a physical exercise program. It helps to clear the mind and keep the body in shape.
- Get adequate rest. It refreshes the mind.
- Pace yourself. Set realistic goals for new challenges. Do not compete with the family or couple next door. Do you.
- Work on your marriage and family relationships.
- Commit yourself to activities that you can accomplish.
- Declutter your schedule and commitments.

ENCOURAGEMENT

Every marriage goes through trying times. Remember the importance of surrounding yourselves with likeminded people who value marriage, especially during the early years of getting know each other. Keep good company.

REFLECTION

#CoupleGoals

DAY 7: DYING PRINCIPLE

When you're married, you have someone who is affected by every decision you make out of selfishness. It's time to die to selfishness and desert your selfish lifestyle.

John 12:24 says, "Most assuredly I say unto you, unless a grain of wheat falls into the ground and dies, it remains alone, but if it does it produces much grain."

Before marriage, you and your spouse were living two separate lives. You were used to a certain routine and doing things when you wanted, how you wanted and with whom you wanted. You made individual decisions. Just getting up and going wherever and doing whatever was the order of the day. Now you must bury that lifestyle and merge to become one. Put away the me, myself, and I attitude. It is painful to be married to someone who functions as if they are single. This independence must be neutralized, leading to the process of the two becoming one. Oneness speaks of unity. No one can come between united people. They cannot be divided. The enemy always wants to sow discord, but we are not ignorant of his devices. Let *Psalm 133:1* become your marriage goal: "Behold how good and how pleasant it is when brethren dwell together in unity." We are married, but we are also brethren in Christ. We do not want to just dwell together, but we aim at dwelling together in unity, harmony, and in agreement as one. The last part of the Psalm shows us the benefit of unity: "There the Lord commands a blessing, life forevermore." The sooner we unite, the sooner we will truly experience the blessing of God together.

Genesis 2:23-25 gives us the blueprint of how God intended us to live together: "Adam said, *'This is now bone of my bones and flesh of my flesh. She shall be called woman because she was taken out of man. Therefore, a man shall leave his father and mother and be joined to his wife and they shall become one flesh. And they were both naked, the man and his wife, and were not ashamed.'"*

One must leave so as to cleave. Leaving one's father and mother does not mean to abandon them, but to realize that the two of you are now a separate, united entity. Your parents can give you advice, but the two of you must decide together whether to implement it. Becoming one is a process we work toward daily. It is a daily commitment. We cannot take a break from each other every time something is not working right; we are in this together.

The marriage vows, "for better for worse, in sickness and in health" are easy to say, but to live them requires determination and unity between spouses. We need to remember that marriage is not to be entered into lightly or unadvisedly; it is not a one-night stand. It's not like impulsively buying a pair of shoes, realizing you don't like them when you get home, and returning them the next day. There is no exchange policy in marriage, so let's work with the "shoes" we got.

Marriage is a lifestyle. As we become one as a couple, we become unstoppable in the kingdom of God. We can rely on the power of agreement. In ***Matthew 18:19, Jesus says, "Again I tell you that if two of you on earth agree about anything they ask for, it will be done for them by my father in heaven."*** My husband and I rely on this power of agreement every time we want to venture into a project, or even in ministry with the challenges we face.

On one occasion, my husband became very excited about a certain business plan, and he wanted to venture into it. Unfortunately, I did not see how we could succeed so I was very reserved in my remarks. Even though he was thrilled with the idea, I was not in agreement. My husband just said, "Honey, would you please find time to pray about it? I prayed and it resonated in my heart that it was the right move." The minute we prayed together in agreement over the capital for the business and the plan, we got a breakthrough. It is advantageous to work together as a team. We are stronger together.

In *1 Corinthians 16:19* and many other New Testament Scripture passages, we find a powerhouse couple named Priscilla and Aquila. This husband and wife team offers us a biblical example of a couple who worked together as one in the kingdom of God and achieved a great amount for His glory.

If you do not make a conscious decision and effort to become one with your spouse, you can easily drift apart. As mentioned earlier, in most developed countries, divorce rates are high among retired people because throughout their working life and years spent raising children, they only focused on their jobs and kids. Now they are both home and retired, the kids have left home, and they realize they have nothing in common. No common friends, no common hobbies. Do not be two strangers under the same roof.

Stan and Lily
Lily came from a well-to-do family and married a middle-class guy. Unfortunately, Lily would sometimes show selfishness, expecting herself, husband, and kids to spend every holiday with her family and for the children to visit her parents, always neglecting her husband's family. Most decisions in her marriage were biased in

favor of the family she came from. Eventually, Stan decided enough was enough and sat her down to talk. It was not easy for her to admit, but she saw his point and heard his cry. They started to visit Stan's parents too, and the paternal grandparents started to enjoy their grandchildren as well.

ACTIVITY

Practical Steps: Exercise on the Dying Principle

- Introspection / Self-evaluation:
  What areas do I need to change?
  In which areas am I selfish?
- What draws us together?
- Make a list of things you enjoy doing together.
- What do we have in common? What shared ground could help us to become one?

ENCOURAGEMENT

We have seen the power of unity in our marriage. This unity enables us to be a resilient team. We are now enjoying the fruit of working together, complimenting each other, and pulling together. We consult one another on decisions small or big. We have learned to value each other's opinions. Where one is blind, the other sees, and where one is deaf, the other hears. What a joy!

REFLECTION

_____

_____

_____

#BecomeOne

DAY 8: ALPHA MALE HIGHEST

Apart from the needs of sex and respect, each husband yearns to be the Alpha male in their spouse's life. This is about giving your husband his place and fulfilling my role as a wife. The following A's are a lot to take on in a day. They can be spread over a time. Nevertheless, we will mention them all today as handy hints and tips to recall when the opportunity presents itself for you to use the wisdom.

A – "Alpha" Hints and Tips to Rub his Ego the Right Way

- Accept him – for who he is, not what he has. Everyone has a weakness, but men thrive where there is acceptance and understanding.

- Appreciate him – for the little and big things.

- Adapt to him – adjust your world and fit into his. Be involved in his hobbies.

- Acknowledge him – in private and public.

- Admire him – even his body. Sometimes you can watch the six-pack grow into a one pack. If this happens, find ways of bringing in diet and exercise.

- Approach him with wisdom – especially when there is a sensitive matter to discuss. The book of Esther in the Bible outlines the successful approach Esther used on the King, who was her husband. She was well heard. The line between respect and disrespect is extremely thin; we should exercise caution.

- Attention – let him take the spotlight in your life. Focus on your man.

- Attend to his needs sexually and intellectually, not just simply giving him food.

- Adore him – love him unreservedly.

- Attract him – men are moved by sight. Always catch his eye. Look good always. Dress, walk, and smell good. Do not stop doing the things that made him chase after you. He must keep pursuing after you. Continue to be breathtaking and not dull.

- Affirm him – words of affirmation boost his ego. When his ego is boosted, he can eat from the palm of your hand.

Danai and Corrie

Danai and Corrie fought often. A major problem was that Danai always felt disrespected and believed Corrie disrespected him and always tried to dominate him in decisions and conversations. When we went to counsel them, Danai said, "Pastors, ask Corrie this question . . . I want to hear her answer. Who wears the pants in this house?" That's the cry of a challenged Alpha male! Corrie, a highly vocal and independent female, had to learn to consider her husband as the leader in their marriage. She learned to submit more and respect him more, and life became exceptionally better for her. She even got a $7,000 ring for their anniversary!

ACTIVITY

Practical Steps: Exercise Regarding the Alpha Male

◆ Rate yourself on how you are doing on each of the above-mentioned A's.

   1. Still at the starting point
   2. Average
   3. Good
   4. Great
   5. Excellent

ENCOURAGEMENT

I do not compare my husband with any other man. I look at him and see God's best masterpiece for me. He is my 'A' man. Be in love with the one you have. Glory to God!

REFLECTION

#LoveHimToBits

DAY 9: PRIORITIZING YOUR SPOUSE

There is a priority order of relationships which guides us and aids us to maintain order in our lives. It goes as follows in order of importance, with the top being the most important:

Priority ladder of relationships:

- God (my personal growth, prayer, fasting, Bible reading)
- Spouse (fulfilling my marital role)
- Family (children) and maybe very close relatives
- Church (programs and any related activities)
- Others

Following this order has assisted me to stay balanced in my Christian walk and as a married woman. Do not leave your marriage at the altar of sacrifice for academic or career success, or anything else, for that matter. Put God first. After God, put each other first. Have godly family values, using the Word of God as a common denominator for the family decisions you make.

Having family traditions for special days like birthdays and wedding anniversaries is particularly important. Know your husband's favorite sports and hobbies. Take a break from outside input. Many times, the gap between a couple can be a consequence of entertaining a lot of outside things and not actually a reflection of your marriage. Therefore, take time to catch up with each other away from any distractions, including children. Find out how your spouse is doing.

Do not allow pride to get in between the two of you. If you are feeling tension or distance, he is probably experiencing it, too. Do not allow it to go on for too long. Prioritize him in your conversations. If you find that your conversations are now kid-based and you communicate through your kids, you need to make change. When did you divorce your husband and marry the kids?

BALANCING OUR LIFE IS CRUCIAL

- We become one by spending time together.
- Spend quality time with your spouse (in prayer, pleasure, pain)
- Make sacrifices to participate in your spouse's hobbies
- Take breaks when possible – short, frequent breaks or a long holiday
- Men bond through sex; women bond through talking. Women need a good listener and a lot of romantic gestures.

Communicate during the day and use social media to your advantage by messaging each other. Life has many pressures. Do not allow the demands of life to cause you to drift apart. Keep bailing excess water out of the boat to ensure that it does not sink.

Willie and Taffy

Taffy seemed to take her hard-working husband for granted. As much as he was looking after her and the children well and giving them an above average lifestyle, she seemed more committed to her friends than to him. She would not treat him well and was not quick to respond to his desires which were fair and straight forward.

While in prayer, my husband Tad saw that if Taffy would not do what Willie had been crying for for a long time, he was moving out. Alarmed, Tad and I phoned Taffy and strongly advised her to prioritize her husband's wishes. Immediately she "suggested" to do what he had been begging her to do for a while—to visit his mother in a neighboring country. She heeded the counsel, phoned him, and he came home immediately to pack so the family could leave for the trip. On their return, Wille confided in Pastor Tad that he had nearly left his wife had she not phoned him agreeing to visit his mom. For the first time, he felt prioritized by his wife.

ACTIVITY

Practical Steps: Exercise on Prioritizing Your Spouse

- In what ways does my spouse view himself as being prioritized?
- Do I put a call on hold and acknowledge him when he walks in the room?
- Do I check with him before making big decisions?
- Do I check with him to make or change plans, or at least inform him?

ENCOURAGEMENT

The hustle and bustle of life can make you put the people you love most last on the list. I recall a time when I got so busy with ministry as a Pastor, attending women's conference after women's conference, that I began to put my husband last. Thank God for a godly man. My husband pointed it out to me and after prayer, I realized he was right. So, before any ministry obligations I make sure I meet his needs first. If I'm going away for a few days, I remember to cook and freeze some meals for him. I am his world.

REFLECTION

#HubbyFirst

DAY 10: LORDSHIP VS. LOVE

My husband and I organize couples retreats as a way of giving couples an opportunity to be refreshed as well as enrich their marriages through teaching. At one of these retreats, I did a research on Lordship vs. Love. Men say, "It is difficult to love someone who does not honor or respect me," while women say, "It's difficult to respect and submit to someone who doesn't love me."

This has been a tug of war that stops many marriages from moving forward. The solution can be found in *Ephesians 5:33 - "Nevertheless let each one of you so love his own wife as himself and let the wife see that she respects her husband."* Show respect and love. When men think that their ego has been rubbed the wrong way or bruised, they find it hard to love. When women feel that they are not being loved, they begin to resent and despise the man, and respect becomes a casualty.

The result is that the relationship comes to a standstill or to a halt. It is a stalemate, and they cannot move forward because each person feels justified to be grieved. Friction, tension, and in some cases, hostility become the order of the day. To get their needs met, some men begin to demand and use force to be heard. You might ask, "How did we get here?" Could it be pride, or simply ignorance?

A relationship is like a living organism. It moves up or in the positive direction if fed the right diet, or down if fed negative actions—and it can only remain stagnant for a while before it shifts in either direction. It can only move up or down. When no one gives in to the other, it means pride has taken over.

Below are some of the answers we received during our research. Using a white board, we asked couples what they view as respect from a man's perspective and love from a woman's perspective. The men wrote on the board taking turns on what they considered respect. In turn, the women also wrote what they considered love.

The following were the results:

Men's views of honor and respect:

Maximum respect to me is:

- When my shirts are ironed, and my clothes are kept tidy.
- When my wife passes something through me before she acts.
- When my wife does not second guess me or counter what I say in front of people or openly support someone who is acting against me.
- When I am not taken for granted in my efforts to improve the family.
- When no matter how heated an argument gets over the phone, she does not cut me off or hang up on me.
- When my ideas and views are acknowledged before being criticized or dismissed as trash or unworkable. I appreciate a mutual conversation or putting on the table better ideas rather than dismissing one's idea without giving much thought.
- When I am talking, and my spouse does not jump into a negative conclusion.
- When she respects my mom for the sacrifices she has made in my life.

Women's views of love:

- I feel loved when he says "I love you" and repeats it throughout the day by text messages or WhatsApp, etc.
- I feel loved when he compliments my appearance.
- I feel loved when he compliments the food I cook
- I feel loved when he puts our relationship first before friends and extended family.
- I feel loved when he shows his loyalty to me as a husband.
- I feel loved when my husband looks after my parents.
- I feel loved when he compliments me on my hard work in my business.
- I feel loved when he pays attention when we are talking.
- I feel loved when he compliments my efforts to lose baby weight.
- I feel loved when he says the words, "I am glad I found you."
- I feel loved when he gives me gifts and surprises me.
- I feel loved when we get quality time together.
- I feel loved when he helps with household chores.
- I feel loved when he cooks and helps with the kids.

The Bible requires women to submit to their own husbands. ***Ephesians 5:22-24 says, "Wives, submit yourselves unto your own husbands, as unto the Lord."*** In the attitude of the heart of submission lies answers to a lot of what men view as respect. Submission has been the most abused word in marriage.

I remember when we were pastoring in Brisbane and the Lord told me to teach the women on submission. All the women said, "NOT that 'S' word again," as if it were a swear word. I had to explain that biblical submission does not mean you are a door mat. It simply means to yield, to give way to his leadership. We have already covered how to respectfully communicate your views and opinions; now allow him to lead.

Men are also commanded by the Word in *Ephesians 5:25 - ". . . that husbands love their wives as Christ loved the church and gave himself for her."* Within a relationship that practices the sacrificial love of Christ, the wife finds it easier to submit. She simply melts in that love and any rough, hard edges are dealt with.

So, who should start first? The love or the respect? My advice is to let each one do their part without eyeing the other. As you graciously do your part, God will give the grace. The solution is in the Word of God. *Ephesians 5:21 says, "Submitting to one another in the fear of God."* This is the key.

Doug and Patricia

Doug and Patricia had come to an uncomfortable impasse in their marriage. When they came to us for counseling, Patricia complained she felt Doug was holding back his love. Doug agreed that it was true and said it was because she was not respecting him enough to deserve his love. I asked Doug what he meant by respect, and he said that to him respect was when Patricia ironed his shirts . . . simple! Patricia promised she would. When we checked in with them later, it was lovey-dovey all the way!

ACTIVITY

Practical Steps: Exercise on Lordship vs. Love

- ◆ Openly discuss what respect means to your husband and what love means to you.
- ◆ Work on ways to meet the most important need to move your marriage in the right direction.

ENCOURAGEMENT

I have learned through experience that I get the best out of my husband when I respect him in the way he views respect. One of his respect languages is that he does not want to be second guessed in front of other people. He always says, "If you are not sure, ask me privately." I have had to learn to give him that respect.

REFLECTION

#GetRidOfPride

11: DO NOT TAKE EACH OTHER FOR GRANTED

*T*aking each other for granted can be something couples do without even realizing it. We should not be so over comfortable with each other that we begin to neglect our relationship. In the second chapter of the Gospel of John, we see Jesus performing His first miracle at a wedding. The couple had run out of wine to serve their guests. Mary, the mother of Jesus, influenced Him to perform His first miracle. When the water turned into wine as the master of the banquet tasted it, the banquet master said, *"Everyone brings out the choice wine first and then the cheaper wine after the guests have had too much to drink; but you have kept the best till now"* *(John 2:10).*

The lesson we may draw from this passage is that in marriage, couples give each other the best of themselves during the early years of marriage; then after some years passed, they begin to serve each other the worst of themselves. We are supposed to get sweeter with age, like wine, as we mature in marriage. We should not become so comfortable with each other that we forget to take care of some of the unspoken rules of marriage, like bathing our bodies, using perfume, and brushing our teeth. Marriage should improve with age, not deteriorate. Do not become complacent and forget the good qualities in your husband that drew you to him.

We should continue to give each other the best of ourselves. I know when kids come, the hectic life of work, business, church, and family sets in, it is easy to begin to neglect what matters most. Sometimes it is the people closest to you that suffer, while other areas prosper. Keep a look out so you are not always giving your spouse the tired, exhausted end of you.

Keep everything in check. If cars need servicing, so does my marriage. If I keep a logbook for my car maintenance, what about my marriage logbook? Do not allow certain good gestures to be overdue, as this can affect everything. Care about your spouse and show that you care. If you just care in your heart and do not show it, that means nothing. Treat each other as vessels of honor as is written in *2 Timothy 2:20*. Honor your spouse in the language he understands.

OUR STORY

The introduction of this book mentions how I had an "intense moment of fellowship" with my dear husband as we drove to a church leadership seminar. I mentioned that we both realized our disagreement was more than what was on the surface. We realized that the major problem was our failure to have enough time to really talk about one or two issues due to our very busy schedules. We had gotten into the mundane stuff of life. We were happy, but there was an issue that needed attention and we realized we had started to take each other for granted a bit. Both of us had things to say, and say them we did. We have resolved that even if our marriage is well, we must just make sure there are no areas whatsoever where we are taking each other for granted.

ACTIVITY

Practical Steps: Exercise for Not Taking Each Other for Granted

◆ Take time to reflect on what you have been serving your spouse.
◆ Do we treat each other as vessels of honor?

- If yes, in what ways?
- If not yet, when and how can you begin?

ENCOURAGEMENT

I must admit, being on one's best behavior for 30 years in a marriage is no walk in the park. All we ask is doing our best to give of our best to each other. It is the little good things we do and the little sweet words we say that mean a lot in marriage.

REFLECTION

#ServeTheBestWineAlways

DAY 12: WITH MY BODY I HONOR YOU

Sex is an integral part of marriage. We should aim to please each other and not being stingy with our bodies, but freely give each other the joy of intimacy.

1 Corinthians 7:3-4 says, "The husband should fulfill his duty to his wife, and likewise the wife to her husband. The wife's body does not belong to her alone but also to her husband. In the same way, the husband's body does not belong to him alone but also his wife."

Surrendering your body to your spouse is one of the most wonderful things the two of you will ever get to share in marriage. This union between husband and wife should be a time of great pleasure, satisfaction, ecstasy, and the adventure of discovering each other's bodies. Hygiene and smelling good is important. Perfume should also be for bedtime and not for going out only. Attract him always and remember, men are moved by sight. I decided to get rid of drab, dull clothes from my wardrobe so that even when I am home doing house chores, I wear something appropriate and not dull and gloomy. I want to catch his eye.

A healthy marriage requires that we fulfill each other's sexual needs, so it is need-based. Do not deprive one another or impose sanctions or rations. Sex is a stressbuster, and research has shown that it improves overall wellness as the body releases endorphins, also known as "the feel-good hormones." So, it has great benefits. Go on and do it.

Physical touch, cuddles, kisses, and massages should be found in abundance between the two of you. Fulfill each other's sexual fantasies. Sexual exploration should be ongoing in marriage, because our bodies are forever changing. As a wife, it is also good and recommended to take charge and lead the act of lovemaking. Women love the act leading up to the intercourse, so let us be in the lead. That way you get the satisfaction of the foreplay. Be in control . . . "torture him" until he calls for his mother! Blow his brains out! Let him think of no other woman but you.

The sexual world is a world we can never exhaust. There are always new tricks and positions; keep exploring and discovering different ways. Do not allow your bedroom life to be predictable and boring. Spice it up with lingerie and fun games. It is stimulating, but some Christians have made it boring. Spontaneous sex is great. Enjoy it together. Any time is fun time. Planned sex is also important. Book a hotel and drop the children at a babysitter or at the grandparents' house. Be intentional. Stress relief sex, otherwise known as a quickie, helps. However, nothing can out do the long play sex.

Make your spouse your "one stop shop" so that there is no need to "shop" elsewhere. Experiment together and discover each other's erotic side. Be romantic. Whisper romantic words to each other. This stimulates the mind, which is the biggest sexual organ. Be clean and hygienic—bath, smell good, brush your teeth, and use perfume.

Create a conducive atmosphere for intimacy in the bedroom. The bedroom is not a courtroom. Put away any unpaid bills and any unfinished work; it kills the mood. Children, including babies and toddlers, should sleep in their own bedrooms. This is about the two of you.

Be faithful to one another. Adultery is one of the worst hurts that a marriage should never have to go through. Bear in mind this Scripture as you journey through marriage: "Marriage is honorable amongst all, and the bed undefiled, but adulterers and fornicated God will judge" (Hebrews 13:4). My body is the best gift I can give to my spouse. Remember, marriage is like an ironing board—if you don't open the legs of the board, you can't iron. So, ladies here we go!

Major Counseling Story

In our over 30 years of counseling, sex issues dominate as much as communication issues do. All our counseling on over four continents reveal that sex is a major issue. A sexless marriage is not a good marriage. I have privately helped many women on how to sexually satisfy their husbands as well as helping them learn how to enjoy sex so much that they begin to instigate it and be really free in bed. Every woman can be a "bedroom athlete" if they put their minds to it. It is not fair for any woman or man to stay sexually starved when they are married. Neither spouse should beg for sex.

ACTIVITY

Practical Steps: Exercise to Honor Your Spouse with Your Body

- ◆ Do you know your husband's sexual fantasies? You cannot fulfill them if you do not know them.
- ◆ Talk about the things that bring the most pleasure in your sex life. Exploration is the most intimate discussion to have. By simply talking about it, you can build intimacy and even raise areas of concern or dissatisfaction and resolve them.

- When did I last fulfill my spouse's sexual fantasy? Be free with your body. Do not be stingy.
- Who initiates sex? Be the aggressor or initiator, too.
- How often do I initiate, be the aggressor, or set the mood and tempo?
- Your man should not have to work hard for sex. If he is the one who initiates all the time, discuss with yourself why you never initiate. Is it fear of rejection? Is it lack of self-confidence? Am I just uninterested? Once you decide why, address it personally and then with your husband.
- Discover what turns him on. We all have triggers. Sex that is sparked by a trigger is most likely able to satisfy both partners.
- What intimate deed does he most appreciate from you?
- Give each other feedback to keep improving the way you satisfy each other.
- Wear his favorite sexy lingerie. Men are moved by sight first, then sex follows. Wear different costumes: maid dresses, fairy princess attire, policewoman uniforms . . . . Playing dress up is fun and getting into the character brings excitement in love making.
- Notice his compliments and keep track of what he likes the most. Also communicate your likes because sex is supposed to be enjoyed by both partners.
- Let your spouse know when they have done well so they can repeat it next time.

ENCOURAGEMENT

As a couple we love trying out new ideas, positions, and playing dress up. We have made a deliberate effort to keep our sexual life exciting and encourage open dialogue to give room for improvement. Sex glues us together.

REFLECTION

#LetsGetItOnBabe

DAY 13: LET'S DO LIFE TOGETHER

'Let's do life together" is our daily motto. Whatever we meet during the day finds us connected. Make a deliberate effort to do life and not allow life to do you. Be proactive about your marriage. It is really about the little beautiful things we share together.

Ecclesiastes 9:9 says, "Live joyfully with the wife of your youth for she is your portion under the sun."

Joy is an inward expression that does not depend on outside influences. Create a conducive atmosphere at home for joy and laughter, even laughing at yourself. Do not be too serious; life is meant to be enjoyed, not endured. Enjoy the simple things in life and celebrate every victory that you experience together. Your spouse is your portion. When you are having a bad day at work, your face should light up when it is time to go home because you look forward to sharing your day with your spouse after work.

Home is a God-given haven. Research has shown that employees who have a safe home and someone to share their life with cope better with the pressures of life. It is true that most men do not really want to talk after a hard day at work, but the fact that they can go home to loving arms and recuperate is a remedy.

Playing together is also restorative. In the Bible we meet Rebecca and Isaac. After Isaac had lied to Abimelech, King of the Philistines, saying that Rebecca was his sister, the way the King saw them showing endearment to each other clearly showed that there was more to their relationship than being brother and sister **(Genesis 26:7-11)**.

Companionship is a key ingredient to a healthy marriage. Be each other's best friend. Life has its up and down moments and a friend close by can comfort, cheer up, and encourage you along the way. There should be a public show of affection that displays the bond between the two of you. Be alive in your marriage; be full of life. It rejuvenates the excitement, which oils the union.

Our marriage goals should be to enjoy the honey throughout your marriage. Where there is honey, there are bees. Learn to focus on how to extract the honey and let the bees do their job. A lot of married people concentrate on the bees instead of finding a way to extract the honey in spite of the bees. Bees here represent the nasty, hurtful things we encounter in life. Honey represents the delightful, pleasant moments of life.

One lady made a sad statement about her marriage after we had shared the above bee analogy. "In my marriage we have no more honey left. In fact, we have killed the bees, too." You must not be complacent while your marriage is dying. Remember, you are the authorized dealer to handle your marriage. Get all the reinforcement that you can to make it healthy.

1 Peter 2:8 says, "Be sober and vigilant, for your adversary the devil roams around like a roaring lion, seeking whom he may devour."

Having date nights refreshes the relationship and brings back the spark. Take longer, proper holidays together with or without the children. Doing life together requires that we stay connected. Do not drop the network.

- Connect emotionally – share thoughts and feelings.
- Connect spiritually – pray and fast together, share Bible readings, etc.
- Connect physically – sex, cuddling, embracing, holding hands, kissing.
- Connect financially – be transparent on money matters.
- Connect throughout the day via WhatsApp, texting, or phoning.
- Develop your own family traditions.

Shad and Bianca

This couple is a perfect example of enjoying marriage. They have adult children now, but even when the kids were younger, they managed to keep a unique routine of date nights, exercising together, going for holidays with and without the kids, and having mind-blowing sex nearly every time. Tad and I have asked this couple now and again to share their success story with other couples. Their unity is amazing.

ACTIVITY

Practical Steps: Exercise on Doing Life Together

- What is your own inside joke that is unique to the two of you?
- Some things are too intimate to mention, so go ahead whisper sweet things to each other.
- Pick your favorite thing to do together that brings you close and is unique to the two of you.
- What is one personality trait your spouse possesses that you are grateful for?

ENCOURAGEMENT

There is no gesture of kindness or love that is too small. One day my husband and I were taking one of our regular walks. He stopped, picked a fresh wildflower, and said to me, "Bae, nice doing life with you." It melted me. Develop a culture of living each day as if it is your last.

REFLECTION

#UsMoments

DAY 14: SURPRISE GIFTS

*E*xchanging of gifts is a great way to show appreciation and affection to your spouse. Gifts simply say, "You are in my thoughts and this is my active way of showing it." Surprise gifts can be small (box of chocolate, flowers, etc.) or big (cars, holiday retreats).

One of the most unforgettable times in my life was when my husband surprised me by bringing my mom to visit us from Africa to Perth, Australia. He organized the visa and bought the tickets secretly. I had no idea as I was busy with a job, ministry, and the children. I went to the airport thinking I was picking up someone else (he said it was a VIP we had been asked to pick up and host for a few days), only to discover it was my own mom. The tears of joy and mixed emotions of excitement and surprise were quite an experience.

That was over 15 years ago but as I write this devotional, I am still filled with the warmth of that joyful experience. It is embedded in my heart forever. He made me feel indebted to return the wonderful, sweet gesture of love. I have tried to outdo my husband, but he is an incurable romantic. I remember when he organized a cruise to the Bahamas for our twenty-third anniversary when we lived and pastored in the USA. I had no idea where we were going.

Some surprises might leave a dent in the wallet. However, they are well worth the smile on your spouse's face and joy in his heart—and above all, the memories created last forever and they help when challenges arise in marriage. Every marriage goes through its testing and trial season. The sweet memories help us to ride out the storms of life hand in hand. This is not a tit for tat exercise, like keeping score or asking, "What has he done for me lately?" This is a gesture of love. Agape love that does good and does not keep score of wrong done.

If we were to equate marriage to a bank account, you cannot withdraw where you did not deposit. If you try, you'll put the account in debt, in the red. Sooner or later, this leads to bankruptcy. There will be no funds available at all. You will max out your cards by your withdrawals without ever depositing. To maintain a healthy marriage, deposit excellent, great things—memories, experiences, and practices—so that during the difficult times you have something to withdraw.

I deliberately mention good surprises because some couples specialize in only giving each other nasty surprises and grief. Sometimes the terrible things just come without much effort because in life, stuff happens. However, for the good surprises we must be intentional. Sometimes being "frugal granny" does not help. Occasionally surprise your husband with that expensive gift that you might think is useless but has much value to him. Save for it and plan. You can source support from friends and family around you to make it a success. Surround yourself with people who value the institution of marriage so that as you prepare the surprise, they support and not sabotage your plans.

Our Couples Retreat Tradition

At least once a year, Tad and I hold Couples Retreats at beautiful, romantic resorts for three days, Friday to Sunday. Tad influences all the husbands attending to secretly buy gifts to present to their wives on Saturday night, which is ballroom night. I also influence all the wives attending to buy gifts and nicely wrap them up for their beloveds. You should see the happiness, joy, and laughter of surprise as couples exchange romantic gifts. Saturday night is always the highlight of the retreat. It is just beautiful. We then encourage all couples to make this a habit and not wait for the retreat.

ACTIVITY

Practical Steps: Exercise on Surprise Gifts
- Search for a gift or something that has been on his heart. It could be a holiday destination, a loved one he has missed . . . think outside the box.
- Is there something he needs, desires, or dreams of? Pay attention to his needs. What does he keep repeating, "I wish I had a . . .?"
- You could ask him to make a wish list or you can write down his wish list as he shares his thoughts, dreams, and aspirations.
- There may be something he really needs that he is afraid to voice out because of a lack of money or fear of your judgement. Is there something he wants that you view as outlandish?
- When did I last surprise my spouse with a well thought out gift?

Food for thought: "Marriages are made in heaven, yes, but they are maintained here on earth."

ENCOURAGEMENT

I have invested in gifts that are expensive and some that are not so pricey. The expression of joy on my hubby's face is always priceless. True, you cannot buy love—but once in love, you can enhance it with good surprises. I believe surprises keep the marriage vibrant.

REFLECTION

#DepositGoodSurprises

DAY 15: AUTHORIZED DEALER

We would be naïve if we do not mention illegal dealers who want to handle your package. Yes, as a married woman I need to be aware that there are other women who want to snatch or steal my dude. I am not saying this for us to go witch hunting or to give your man an excuse not to exercise self-control. However, in the world we are living in, there are some women with no respect for the institution of marriage or the fact that your man is married and has a ring on his finger.

The wisdom which we will share here reminds me of the day a certain lady walked into church during the food fellowship after the service and began to speak with my husband in a suggestive manner. She was hitting on him. We were pastoring the church in Brisbane, Australia at the time. Everything in me was screaming to "hug her by the throat," but thank God for teachings on self-control. I went and stood next to my husband, smiling and fixing his collar (which did not need fixing). I was marking my territory. I did not say a word.

Rule number one, ladies: be secure in your relationship. I am the one he married, and that gives me the confidence to not be chasing after him all the time but to do my part as his wife and trust God to protect him. Several women put so much strength and energy into trying to find out who their man has been talking to even at the office, that it becomes a distraction from focusing on how to keep him.

Where trust has been broken, work on rebuilding it. To be looking over your shoulder every time he goes away is not healthy for you or the relationship. We need to mention again the need to be forgiving. We are not talking about someone who is a habitual adulterer, but maybe he slipped once, and you decided to forgive and go ahead with the marriage. You did well, now let us focus and work on rebuilding the marriage. Get help in counseling and prayer to get over the painful and rough patch.

God gave us as women the exact same body parts. There is no woman with extra or spare body parts elsewhere. Therefore, let us be confident in the way we have been made. In addition, let us make use of what we have. Give him the sex he desires. We also need to be careful not to push away our husbands by throwing words of accusation at them. The saying is true that "women know women," and we can see a woman of loose morals preying on our husbands before he himself realizes what's happening. Warn him, but do not blame him. The fact that as women we can smell a "sister" of loose morals from afar does not mean our husbands can.

This reminds me of what happened when we were in the USA. A certain couple came in for counseling and the wife was fuming and complaining about the husband's conduct with a female work colleague. He had not fallen into sin, but she feared that the lady was giving him too much attention. The husband was quite oblivious to this fact, so we warned the man to be aware and alert. He was so oblivious of the woman's advances that he thought his wife was nagging.

Then when they had an office Christmas party, the female colleague was not expecting him to come with his wife, but he did. When she saw the wife, she was angry and literally blurted out what she had been planning and plotting: on that very day, come hell or thunder, she was going to sleep with him. She had intended to seduce him that night. Thank God the husband had listened to our advice, and the wife was vigilant and handled the matter with wisdom.

Here are some things to look out for:

- If there is a spirit of lust or iniquity that runs in his blood, it needs deliverance. Enlist the help of your pastor.
- Not being unwise or vigilant with members of the opposite sex; flirting
- Lying to each other – little lies tend to grow and become big. Scripture reminds us that the devil is the father of lies. The devil works in darkness, so be honest with one another.
- Making a habit of resenting, despising, mocking, or belittling your spouse – you cannot enjoy him. He becomes undesirable in your eyes, which can lead to destroyed intimacy.
- Keeping dark secrets – the devil operates best in darkness, and negatives are processed in the dark. Transparency and openness keep us from his trap.
- Poor conflict resolution – allowing things to pile up. They become the trigger that blows all hell loose, or as we say, "the straw that broke the camel's back."
- Lack of intimacy – this creates a timebomb, as sex is a basic need and lack of it leads to frustrations and opens negative doors.
- Sexual indiscipline including dabbling in pornography – this makes you begin to compare that with your spouse. Yes, there are women who indulge in pornography. It is like bringing a ghost into the sanctuary of your bedroom. Keep your sexual life pure.

Taffy and Gugulethu
Taffy was a nice guy but had the weakness of floundering. He happened to be a real hunk, so many women were after him. This caused a lot of angst and demoralization to Gugu. So, we sat them down. It happened that Taffy had a remarkably high sex drive and was embarrassed to let his wife know, so he would end up getting attention elsewhere. Gugu stepped up and told him that there was nothing she could not handle. She assured him that whenever he wanted a cuddle, an embrace, or sex, she would always be ready for him. She was going to be his "one-stop shop." She told him she was game any day, any time, and so he need not look anywhere else. She was going take care of all his fantasies and be her husband's exclusive "authorized dealership." That settled it and stabilized that relationship!

ACTIVITY

Practical Steps: Exercise to Deal with My Man

◆ Be open about any women who might be trying to hook up with your man and work out a way to keep them out.
◆ Be vigilant, alert, and attentive to the needs of your marriage. As the Americans say, "Handle your business, sister!"

ENCOURAGEMENT
Transparency and integrity are rare qualities and must be treasured, or at least we must endeavor to achieve. Allow yourself to be accountable to each other.

REFLECTION

#AuthorisedDealerOnly

DAY 16: SELF-CARE

One day I saw a vision of a lady juggling a lot of balls with the words wife, mom, sister, daughter-in-law, daughter, businesswoman, chief executive officer, lawyer, nurse, doctor, pastor . . . the list was endless. I saw the lady managing to catch all these balls without dropping one. She had the skills to multitask and fulfill all that was required of her. However, I saw a ball that had been crushed on the floor. She struggled to pick it up, and ignored it until it was beginning to affect the flow of the other balls she was juggling. The ball on the floor had the word, SELF-CARE.

Isn't it amazing that when you board a flight, the safety video instructs you that in the event of pressure falling, you should put your oxygen mask on first before you help someone next to you? As women, by nature we care and put everyone else first, whether the needs are physical, emotional, social, or practical. With so much to take care of, we sometimes forget or neglect to take care of ourselves.

Bear in mind that we are only as good as the way we feel in any relationship. Your body is the vehicle that carries you on earth. Pamper yourself. Go for that manicure or pedicure, hairdresser appointment, or facial treatment; it will revitalize you. Everything should be done in moderation. Self-care requires us to be watchful of what we eat, including the nutritional value of our meals and correct size portions. Taking regular walks or any form of exercise should be our lifestyle. It assists in keeping us healthy. We are only as good as the way we feel.

We also need to adhere to regular health check-ups, including pap smears, mammograms, and blood tests. Take whatever medication you are prescribed by doctors faithfully. Get a doctor's clearance before you just decide to stop medication on your own.

Mental Coping Mechanisms

In places where we have housemaids to help us around the house to cope with housework, we must always remember, the maid is my helper and I am my husband's helper. Therefore, anything he wants, he comes to me. If I instruct the maid to assist me to prepare a meal, it is my hand that hands over the food to my husband. Men naturally give attention to the hand that feeds them or irons their shirt or helps them with the little things. In self-care I may get assistance, but I use wisdom and caution.

In other places, however, maids are a luxury that is just dreamed of and can never be afforded. In these cases, one needs to engage coping mechanisms to juggle everything without being overwhelmed. My husband and I once visited a lady who had just had her third baby, but she looked well, youthful, and well rested. The house was clean, everything neatly packed away, and I asked her how she was managing. She had adapted what I will call "coping mechanisms." She had employed a cleaner to do the difficult cleaning twice a month in her house. That enabled her to do light cleaning during the other days which was not back breaking. This gave her strength to deal with the other pressures.

Yes, I know hubby can help, but enlist outside help if you are drowning. Get someone to just come deal with the pile of laundry or scrub the bathrooms and clean the windows if it will help you to rest. Allow some down time by decluttering your schedule. Soak yourself in the tub or take a hot shower. If you use the bucket method for your bath, use extra buckets of water. Even God rested on the seventh day after creating the earth. We are not talking about being lazy, but for genuinely hard-working women, take a breather. To all the hard-working women reading this devotional, you are an unsung hero and today I truly salute you. Do not wait until you are crushed from exhaustion. Take sizeable bits with the responsibilities you shoulder. Remember, some of your energy must go into your sex life, so leave some for your husband.

Organization is key; it saves you time. Little things like picking your outfit the night before a big day and double checking to see that it still fits will save you stress in the early morning rush. During the time our children were still under our roof, I would cook meals and freeze them so the kids could just warm up their food after school. Ladies, you know how it is during childbearing and child rearing. Funny how that is usually the time a lot of marriages suffer.

There was a time when we were living in the USA that I went and bought several pairs of the same color socks for my son. He kept crying about not being able to find matching socks almost every morning. He is the fussy type that will not wear two different color socks. Do what works. Be kind to yourself; do not compare yourself with anyone. You are unique. Laugh at yourself for some of the mistakes and forgive yourself for the wrongs done.

Get the REVELATION that you that are the apple of God's eye:

R - Read daily
E - Examine your life
V - Value your time
E - Exercise faith, exercise your body

L – Love, live, and always laugh
A – Adore and acknowledge God
T – Thank the Lord for His kindness
I – Immerse yourself with inspiration and intimacy with God
O – Organize your life
N – Never quit

Take time to meditate on Psalm 139.

Jill's Story

Jill had just had a new baby, making it three kids under four! Due to this workload her self-care deteriorated, and she ended up neglecting herself to the extent of cutting her own hair. Maybe grooming it had become a challenge. I shared with her how she could involve her husband in taking care of the other two children, and he was quite obliging. She had to outsource help here and there, and thank God her husband stepped in big time so that she was no longer feeling like she was underwater, just aiming to survive. Her bounce, joy, and sense of wellbeing shot up and she was her incredibly beautiful self again.

ACTIVITY

Practical Steps: Exercise for Self-care

- Keep a diary of any due medical check-ups and book for all GP appointments.
- Know what helps you to relax.
- Do not ignore any warning signs in your body.
- Avoid stress.

ENCOURAGEMENT

My sister, you cannot stay on earth without a body. Take time to keep it healthy and groomed. It is also the vehicle that carries you and allows you to communicate your love to the world. Let us look after ourselves.

REFLECTION

#SelfCare

DAY 17: FROM IN-LAWS TO IN-LOVES

*S*how kindness to your in-laws and turn them into "in-loves." It is true what they say, that when you get married you are marrying into a family and every family is different. While I am still learning and getting to know my new family, I must find a way of dwelling with them in peace as the Bible requires.

Romans 12:18 says, "If it is possible as much as it depends on you, live at peace with all men."

Your husband did not fall from heaven; therefore, it is important to respect the family he was raised in. It is also vitally important to demystify the notion that daughters-in-law and mothers-in-law do not get along. In any relationship, attitude is everything. One should not enter marriage ready to kick their husband's mom out of his life. We both play different, important roles in his life. He can have sufficient, different love for both of us.

There is no need to compete with one another. I ought to appreciate my mother-in-law for the work she did in birthing and raising him up. After all, she is the one who worked hard to discipline him and instill in him the attributes that I now enjoy. She played a part in his life that I can never play nor take away from her. Therefore, it is not my role to talk about her shortcomings or her faults.

My role is to promote unity in the family and not join into negative conversations about members of the family. Blood is thicker than water. They can talk about each other and forgive each other, but once I add my two cents of negative words, it is viewed in a different light.

Maybe you have been married for a while and the struggles are real between you and your mom-in-law. It is of no benefit to you to label her the "monster-in-law." Instead, speak positively—she is my mom-in-love. I fell in love with my handsome man (her son) and she came with the package. Be encouraged to do good. Where you have made any mistakes, correct them and move forward. You may need to correct any damage you have contributed and leave the rest to God.

The vows that we now declare at weddings between husband and wife were actually first shared between mother-in-love and daughter-in-love. In the Bible, the book of Ruth records, "***Entreat me not to leave you or turn back from following you; for where you go, I will go and where you lodge, I will lodge. Your people shall be my people and your God shall be my God***" *(Ruth 1:16-17)*.

Such was the bond between Ruth and Naomi her mother-in-law that they looked after each other long after the death of Naomi's son, Ruth's husband. Their connection as women was solid. If we as women come together, we can positively influence the men in our lives. We must be intentional in reaching out and checking in on our mother-in-love or visiting where possible. For Ruth and Naomi, they became friends. Ruth means "friendly" or "friendship." After all, as women, our struggles are similar. Fearing whether they accept you or whether you will fit into the family can only be overcome with time and taking the right action as situations arise. After a while you advance from being daughter-in-law to daughter, then after some years you become a mother in that family.

I recall the time I got married. It was a bit of a rough start with my mother-in-love. However, I reminisced on the teaching I had received from a lady's group I had attended. The lesson was, "She is your mother, and every mother needs respect. You must get to know her." After some years of prayer and intentional actions to build a healthy relationship, we became best friends. It took effort and a lot of forgiving of each other. On my part, after I had my first son, I decided that this relationship must be sweet. I needed to work on improving it because one day my son will also marry, and I too will be a mother-in-law. There was great need to sow good seeds.

Just as a rule of thumb, do not make a habit of pointing out to your husband every little thing that is wrong with his family. It destroys him because he can neither fix the whole family nor reject them. When you tell a man something, they want to fix it—but this is the one thing that at times just cannot be fixed, so instead it adds frustration and strains your relationship. Pick your battles where there is genuine concern affecting your family, then revisit the communication rules and talk about it in a respectful manner, being careful not to accuse or blame anyone. There is also no perfect family, by the way—even on your side. Every man feels good when they know you accept their family as yours, which is the goal in marriage.

Eugene and Ropa
Eugene and Ropa were sweethearts who had met in college. All was well until Eugene's mother and sisters began to interfere in their marriage. They overstepped big time to the extent of doing Eugene's laundry while Ropa was there. Eugene was the last born, and whenever he and his wife had a small misunderstanding, he

would rush to report to his siblings, who thought their little brother, the baby of the family, was suffering. This created ill feelings between them and Ropa, who obviously thought they were indicating that she was an incapable wife and housekeeper.

When Eugene and Ropa came to us for help, we advised Eugene to tell his folks not to interfere with his marriage and for him to stop reporting his marital disagreements to them. Also, Ropa had to find a way to tell her in-laws that she loved them but interfering with her housekeeping just wasn't on. It worked!

ACTIVITY

Practical Steps: Exercise for Living with In-laws

Show kindness consistently in words and deeds
- Phone or text a family member to just check up on them
- Help them financially when they are in need
- Do not separate your husband from his brothers
- Allow your in-laws to visit you

ENCOURAGEMENT

Falling in love is a wonderful thing, and it comes with a wonderful new family who become our family, too. Embrace them. Speak with wisdom. Take time to study them.

REFLECTION

_____

_____

#YourPeopleShallBeMyPeople

DAY 18: VIEWING HIM THROUGH THE WORD

*T*he world we live in today has made a mockery of men and presented them as slow or incompetent. Movies have been made in which the father figure in the house is presented as retarded or an idiot. Portraying men as dysfunctional basically demasculinizes them. Some women even vocalize it on different platforms, barraging men probably because of probably what they have gone through caused by a bad father or some other harmful male figure in their life. But all men are not the same. We want to take the measure of a man from the Word of God, because He is the One who created the first male in the Garden of Eden.

Your husband is the priest and spiritual leader in the home.

Let's consider the following roles your husband plays:

Priest:

According to *1 Peter 2:9, by God's order men are to lead in spiritual matters in the home*. This includes prayer, tithing, and study of the Word. He is the head, and the head is supposed to lead in everything. In Scripture we refer to the God of Abraham, Isaac, and Jacob. The ideal home should be patriarch-led, not matriarch-led. As a wife, when I sense that we can do better in prayer, fasting, or Bible study in the home, I can use my influence to influence the family into a deeper spiritual walk. Keep in mind that men do not always pray in the same way as women with a lot of emotion and noise. Therefore, do not judge him. Praying strengthens the vertical relationship we have with God and in turn oils our horizontal relationships.

Provider:

Genesis 2:15 says, "The Lord God took the man and put him in the garden of Eden to work it and take care of it." God gave man work before a wife. We are living in a generation where women are also working and earning an income, sometimes more than the man. He may be making less money, but he is still the provider. What the wife brings in is also to be appreciated, but the fact is that even if a woman earns more, she would like to enjoy the money her husband gets. A prudent woman will keep encouraging the husband and show gratitude for all his efforts in providing for the family. This encourages him to achieve more.

Protector:

I personally feel a sense of safety when I have a male figure around. A good man protects his wife—physically, emotionally, spiritually, and in social circles. Allow him to protect you. Personally, I would not open the door if there is a knock and my husband is home, even when I know who is at the door. Let my protector answer the door . . . just in case! We know ultimately that God is our protector, but men have also been given the responsibility to protect their family.

Promise Keeper:

He is a promise keeper, firstly of the marriage vows, then any other promises made later. Is he a man of his word? Am I able to take his word to the bank? Is he a man of integrity, honesty, and truth? These are qualities that give women peace of mind in the marriage.

Pleasure Giver:

Being playful with one another keeps the relationship young and alive. As mentioned previously, Isaac was caught expressing a public show of affection to his wife (Genesis 26:7-8). It is important to have fun moments together.

Ecclesiastes 8:9 says, "Live joyfully with the wife whom you love all the days of your vain life which He has given you under the sun, all your days of vanity; for that is your portion in life, and in the labor which you perform under the sun." Enjoy him each day.

Planner:

Faith is not a substitute for lack of planning. As a family we need to have short and long-term plans. The husband is the leader in this area. He is the visionary, and as a wife I implement whatever we have agreed on the plan. There is power in agreement as a couple.

Producer:

Genesis 1:28 says, "And God blessed them and said to them, 'Be fruitful and multiply . . . ."
Genesis 9:1 says, "And God blessed Noah and his sons and said to them, 'Be fruitful and multiply and fill the earth."'

We are called to be fruitful in our marriage, not just in childbearing also financially and materially. There should be increase in all areas of our life.

Prophet:

Men need to prophesy over their children and wives and speak into their destiny. Jacob, the great patriarch, spoke life into his son when Rachel had spoken negatively because of the childbearing pain she suffered in delivering him. A father can prophesy good upon his child and change the course of negative events. For example, Rachel called her son Benoni (son of my sorrow), but Jacob prophesied and called him Benjamin (son of my strength). Out of him came the first king of Israel, because the father prophesied. His tribe also became renowned warriors, left-handed experts of the bow and arrow. Jacob later prophesied on all his sons (***Genesis 49***).

If my husband is not yet there in all the "P's" mentioned above, as a prudent woman I continue to view him through the Word of God until it molds him. I do not compare him to other men or confront him. I confess what the Word says he is. The Word will always prevail.

Sam and Adiah

We got to know this couple through a fellow countryman who introduced us. Sam was much older than his wife Adiah. However, Adiah's respect for Sam was very poor, and she would address him any how and call him all sorts of names—sometimes jokingly, yet it was still bad. These two got born again, and through Women's Ministry teachings Adiah's attitude toward her husband changed and she started to honor her husband as a man of God. In turn, Sam became more responsible and they both matured in faith and in their relationship. They are now outstanding leaders in the church.

ACTIVITY

Practical Steps: Exercise for Viewing Him Through the Word

- Confess the Word of God in prayer and over your husband
- See the Word fulfilled in your spirit until it manifests
- Gently encourage your husband and be his best cheerleader
- Encourage him to keep company with godly men, men of spiritual stature

ENCOURAGEMENT

Allow the Word of God, not the world, to mold your husband. Pray and speak the Word over every aspect of his life.

REFLECTION

#MyPleasureGiver

DAY 19: DIFFERENT WIRING

Wired differently from us

Your husband is not difficult to understand. Just study how he thinks and master him. Men are simple; their basic needs are not as complicated as a woman's. It is important to learn how to meet your husband's needs, so take time to discover him. Bear in mind that our husbands are not like our girlfriends; they are wired differently. If I go shopping with my girlfriend, we cheerfully go from shop to shop, try out different things like perfume, make up, and clothes, and compare different shops before we buy. We will both be happy and excited about doing that. Most men, however, when you convince them to go shopping with you are usually quite content to sit at a bench or go into a coffee shop, read the newspaper, or scroll on the phone while you shop. Ladies, let us not expect them to behave like us. We are wired differently. Men shop like they have blinkers—get into one shop and out with the product! Well, it might take the fun out of shopping, but that is what makes them men— singular focus!

Women have a lot of wires in their heads; that is how we can do many things at once. Our brains are like the Internet. We can juggle a lot of things at one time. Men tend to think in compartments. Men are also not as expressive as women. They do not want to feel vulnerable. This can cause a measure of insecurity in them as they can easily get frustrated, angry, withdrawn, bitter, or withhold love if they have some unmet needs. Find out where he thinks his needs are not being met. Figure out a way to fulfill the realistic needs because unmet needs have negative consequences. Met needs lead to openness and confidence, and he in turn will strive to also satisfy your needs.

Proverbs 31:11-12 says, "The heart of her husband safely trusts her, so he will have no lack of gain. She does him good not evil all the days of her life." The good she does includes comfort, support, and reassurance. Call the king out of your husband and the king will manifest! Men are wired to appreciate beauty. Look good always, because you are the Queen. Every king has a queen.

Ladies, we have the power to declare and decree the king to come out of our husbands by what we speak and how we address them. As I praise his achievements, he begins to believe in himself and works harder to provide and be a better husband and father to the family. Do not cross the line between friendship and husband. This is a fine line that can be easily crossed. I should not second guess or undermine his leadership and authority in the house. Cover his nakedness and weaknesses. Show him respect and do not expose him. Be his number one supporter and cheerleader. Prosper together with your husband. Encourage your husband when he goes off to work. In some workplaces there are female bosses bossing him around all day, so when he comes home, he wants to feel like the king in a palace even if the palace is one room. When he is at home, do not demean him. Build your man up by your words.

Remember, because a man is wired to be able to put things in different compartments in his head, he acts differently. Has your husband asked you for sex immediately after an argument? Yes, that is how a man operates. While you are still fuming and trying to calm down, he has put the argument, solved or unsolved, into a compartment and locked it. Now he is ready and raring to go sex-wise and you think, "Really? Is he for real?" Yes, my dear, he is very real!

Women, on the other hand . . . our wires are beautifully connected all over in our cute heads, and one thing triggers everything else! Consequently, the argument, the emotions, and all these things may cause me not to want anything to do with sex. Meanwhile, hubby is even surprised . . . "What does our 'intense moment of fellowship' have to do with our bedroom life?" As women, we bunch it all together and that is why in an argument, we bring in all the history from past experiences into the argument and other things better described as "off topic." In our heads, however, it's all together. We are wired differently, and that is what brings the excitement in marriage when we grasp it.

Our Story

This is still ongoing! Many times I ask my husband to do things exactly my way or vise versa, and it doesn't work. We don't fight about it anymore, but once in a while he seems to forget I am a woman and expects me to jump out of the car as soon as he stops. Over thirty years later, he is still amazed that I take five minutes to eventually gather myself and all that's mine and get out of the car . . . gracefully! He has learned to be patient, but he still laughs and teases me about it. On the other hand, I laugh at his ability to zone out into space and watch TV without seeing or hearing what's being said. He is normally elsewhere in another little box in his head. I sometimes have to get his attention and then maybe repeat something before we are together. When I ask him where he has been, he tells me of things to be done, problems to solve, and people to contact! Really? In the middle of watching a movie together! That's men for you – wired totally different!

ACTIVITY

Practical Steps: Exercise for Understanding How You are Wired Differently

Compare your different wiring in:

- Shopping
- Story telling
- Planning a holiday
- Preparing to go to an important meeting

Discuss the different compartments your husband has in his head. Allow him to guide you through a serious discussion when you begin to bundle up things together.

ENCOURAGEMENT

Incorporate your differences, and remember, that is what attracted you to each other. Work on using those differences to complement each other, not repel one another.

REFLECTION

_____

_____

_____

_____

_____

_____

#DifferentWirringIsFun

DAY 20: KEEP SWEET MEMORIES ALIVE

On one of our couples group forums, we gave a challenge for couples to post old photos of themselves together. This brought such an excitement amongst the couples and made me realize that married people need reminders of sweet memories along the way. I then wrote the following poem from that experience:

OUR MEMORIES OF "YESTER-YEAR"

Remember the days of old when you fell in love
Remember how you did not have much in terms of material things
But only the promise of love
Remember how you would exchange smiles from afar in a crowd
Remember how you would look forward to seeing each other even for just a few minutes
Remember how it would hurt to say goodbye after each date
Remember how you would dress your best, smell your best, behave your best . . . "best foot forward"
Remember . . . Remember
Now a few years have gone by
We have journeyed together a while
In life "stuff happens"
In life "life happens"
Remember . . . remember
Remember what brought you together
That is the glue that will keep you together—so remember

The children of Israel were instructed by God to keep the memories alive, lest they forget. They were told to pile stones together that would be a reminder of what God had done for Israel. *Joshua 4:6 says, "The stones will be a reminder to you when your children ask someday,* 'Why are these stones important to you?'" Going down memory lane rekindles the fire. It is important to reminisce on the days of yester-year. Remember where the Lord has taken you from and where the Lord has placed you now, lest we forget to thank Him for the grace in our marriages. Deuteronomy 6:12 says, "Then beware, lest you forget the Lord who brought you out of the land of Egypt, from the land of bondage." Do not forget how God brought you together. Draw strength from pleasant memories.

Petronella's Story

Petronella, a very loving mother and wife, lost the love of her life through a long illness. She was indeed devasted. As we tried to console her, I realized even more how much she loved her recently deceased husband. I asked her where and how they had met. Straight away, her face lit up, and she started to narrate every detail of their love story. All the sweet memories flooded back, and she was able to handle the grief better. That day, I realized once again the importance of creating sweet memories.

ACTIVITY

Practical Steps: Exercise to Keep Sweet Memories Alive

- ◆ Keep a record of good memories
- ◆ Pull out old videos and photos or view them on any device
- ◆ Play a "Do You Remember?" game as you share the memories
- ◆ Take turn turns talking about the joyous events that you have experienced together

- See whether you remember how and where you spent Christmas holidays since you got married
- Reminisce on past wedding anniversaries and children's births
- Celebrate any milestones, graduations, business success, and promotions in life

ENCOURAGEMENT

Marriage is a journey that has both bitter and sweet memories. On any journey, you can choose to look at the beauty and focus on the positives. My husband and I have had times we cried together and laughed together. We choose to make our conversations center around the times we have laughed together, as this is where we draw our strength.

REFLECTION

#MemoriesAreForKeeps

DAY 21: QUITTING IS NOT AN OPTION

*S*ong of Solomon 3:4 says, "Scarcely had I passed by them, when I found the one I love. I held him and would not let him go, until I had brought him to the house of my mother."

You have come this far, Ebenezer; thus far the Lord has brought us. This is a day of reflecting on victories won, rivers crossed, and mountains climbed. Champions may fail, but they certainly never quit. Do not quit. Fight for your promised land. It is there for you.

Marriage is a journey with difficult terrains and different seasons, but you will succeed if you put your marriage on the unmovable rock, Jesus Christ. The mountains climbed, the tough terrain navigated, the valleys crossed, the low moments elevated, the potholes navigated, the ditches leaped over, and the unexpected rough times conquered are all a sign of our love and determination. At the end of it all, that which did not kill us can only make us stronger. The rainy days drizzled and the foggy weather was dark, but we remained standing. The sunny days and the joyous days spent together keep us smiling.

Never give up on your marriage. Never quit! Good friends are important, couples or women of like mind who hold the institution of marriage in high regard and sacredness. Surround yourself with people of likeminded conviction. Determine that your marriage will not be a statistic for failure. If it depends on me as a woman or wife, I will do my utmost to make it work. Take care of your business, sister! Keep polishing that diamond in your hands; one day you will see the sparkle.

ACTIVITY

Practical Steps: Exercise for Not Quitting

"Of Course You Can" (OCYC)

Here are some Of Course You Can (OCYC) words of encouragement:

OCYC receive great revelation about your life
OCYC fly higher than an eagle
OCYC achieve greatness
OCYC more than make it
OCYC prosper
OCYC succeed
OCYC move in miracles, signs, and wonders
OCYC move in the gifts of the Spirit
OCYC drive that dream car
OCYC live in that beautiful mansion
OCYC get a higher education
OCYC live your dreams
OCYC go on your dream vacation
OCYC enjoy your inheritance
OCYC have the most beautiful marriage

Continue this phrase with your own words.

Sometimes you just need to look at the woman in the mirror and remind her: Woman, of course you surely can!

ENCOURAGEMENT

The Lord be gracious to you, woman of God. When all is said and done, trust in the Lord always. May He pour the Abraham and Sarah blessing upon you—the blessing that conquers any adversity thrown at you and the blessing of longevity together.

REFLECTION

#VictoryIsMine
YesICan

Books by Tadius and Gwen Mawoko

- CROSS-CULTURAL MISSION WORK AND CHURCH PLANTING
  Memoirs of a Young Missionary Couple – by Tadius Mawoko

FUTURE BOOKS AND SERVICES

- YOUR MARRIAGE – HEAVEN OR HELL ON EARTH? (Coming Soon)
  by Tadius Mawoko

AUTHOR CONTACT INFORMATION

Email: gwen@tadandgwen.com
Website: www.tadandgwen.com
Facebook: Pastor Gwen Tendayi Mawoko

ISBNs for this Book

ISBN: # (paperback) 978-0-6450145-0-1
ISBN: # (hardback)   978-0-6450145-1-8
ISBN: # (epub)   978-0-6450145-2-5

ACKNOWLEDGMENTS

Firstly, I would like to acknowledge my wonderful husband and love of my life, Dr. Tad, whose unmatched support made this project possible. You have been my encourager, supporter, pastor, prayer partner, friend, and lover. You are an amazing husband, family administrator, provider, and excellent father to our children, the 3B's! I thank God for the incurable romantic you are! We have been through everything together. Doing life with you has been an amazing adventure in God. I love you deeply.

I also want to acknowledge Rudo Mutsigwa and Pastor Rudo Rwizi for the hard work in editing this book with Belinda and Dr. Tad. Rudo Mutsigwa. You were tireless!

My mom, the late Pastor Milcah Ndleleni Samasuwo—you have gone to glory, but not forgotten. Your disciplining, teachings, prayers, and counsel especially in the early years of my marriage have borne fruit.

Lastly but not least, to the best spiritual parents ever, Archbishops Apostles Drs. E.H & E. Guti. Your patience with me, your love, and your prayers have not been in vain. I love you so much and continue to intercede for you! Long life to the greatest father and mother! I am so proud to be your daughter.

Above all, to God the Father who, by His Spirit, inspired me to write this devotional. Jesus, my Savior . . . You are beautiful!

ABOUT THE AUTHOR

Pastor Gwendolene Nothando Tendayi Mawoko, better known simply as Dr. Gwen, is a wife and mother, a pastor, a marriage and premarital counselor, an intercessor, and a motivational speaker. She is a former Travel Agent and Safari Consultant who worked for an airline and later Safari Companies in Zimbabwe prior to going into the ministry with her husband. She has also worked for two airlines in Australia while co-pastoring churches there. Dr. Gwen holds IATA Diplomas in Travel and Tourism, a diploma in theology from AMFCC, a bachelor's and Master's in Biblical Studies and a Doctorate in Ministry from FICU, California, USA. She also holds a Certificate in Advanced Counseling from Christ for the Nations Institute (Dallas, TX) (where she was also a guest tutor), and a Graduate Certificate in Education Studies from Monash University in Melbourne, Australia, and has embarked on a Masters in Counseling with Monash University. She and her husband, Pastor Tadius Mawoko, have been missionaries to several countries since 1997. They started counseling married couples 30 years ago, a year into their own marriage, and have witnessed tremendous results. As a speaker at conferences and marriage seminars, Dr. Gwen is known to move in the prophetic and for her dry humor in applying the Word of God. Drs. Tad and Gwen are blessed with three children, Bethel, Bethany, and Belinda, who by God's grace are all accounted for in the Lord.

www.ingramcontent.com/pod-product-compliance
Lightning Source LLC
Chambersburg PA
CBHW050819090426
42737CB00021B/3441